# LOS ANGELES UNCOVERED

## Frank Thompson

Seaside Press

Library of Congress Cataloging-in-Publication Data

Thompson, Frank T., 1952-.
    Los Angeles uncovered    / Frank Thompson.
        p.        cm.
    Includes index.
    ISBN 1-55622-391-9  (pbk.)
    1. Los Angeles (Calif.)—Description and travel.     2. Los Angeles
(Calif.)—History.     3. Los Angeles (Calif.)—Guidebooks.     I. Title.
    F869.L84T46      1995
    917.94'930453—dc20
                                                                    95-14522
                                                                    CIP

Copyright © 1996, Frank Thompson

All Rights Reserved

ISBN 1-55622-391-9
10  9  8  7  6  5  4  3  2  1
9507

All inquiries for volume purchases of this book should be addressed to
Wordware Publishing, Inc., at 1506 Capital Avenue, Plano, Texas 75074.
Telephone inquiries may be made by calling:

(214) 423-0090

*Dedicated to*
*Angelyne*
*The spirit of Los Angeles incarnate*

# Table of Contents

# Contents

Contents

# Introduction

Just a few years ago, I had a defining Los Angeles moment. I hadn't moved here yet, although I had decided to do so in the near future, but had come out for a few months to work on a television series based on Kenneth Anger's *Hollywood Babylon*. (Don't blame the finished product on me! I'm innocent!) I was to return to Boston on a Saturday in April, but on the Wednesday preceding my departure, the verdict was pronounced in the Rodney King trial. Within hours, Los Angeles was in the grip of terror, rocked with riots, fire, violence. I came to work the next morning, but no one in our Wilshire Avenue building got anything done. All eyes were glued to the television sets, where grinning, armed gang members were shouting to the camera, "We're going to Beverly Hills!" Since we were *in* Beverly Hills at the moment, it seemed prudent to go elsewhere. By noon, I was driving over the hill toward my apartment. I'm probably the only person in history who ever fled to Van Nuys for safety.

That night, I sat in my little second-story studio, scanning the horizon, feeling like Davy Crockett at the Alamo, waiting for the final assault to begin. As I tried to go to sleep, I began wondering whether moving to Los Angeles would be such a good idea after all.

The next morning, I got a call from my good friend Tom, who—to his regret—was also involved with *Hollywood Babylon*. "Hey Frank," he said, "I have to go down to the Beverly Hills Hotel today. We're still filming the Tony Curtis intros. Want to come with me?" Tony Curtis was the host—I'm sure, to *his* regret, too—of *Hollywood Babylon*. I didn't see any reason to remain locked in an apartment in Van Nuys all day so I said, "Sure."

As we drove along Mulholland Drive and then down Coldwater Canyon into Beverly Hills, we could see the smoke from the riot fires in the distance. Otherwise everything seemed normal. Quiet, but normal.

Within the hour, Tom and I were sitting by the pool of a $3,000-a-day bungalow at the Beverly Hills Hotel, sipping margaritas and chatting with Tony Curtis, who was dressed in white tennis togs. The smoke was still rising from the riot fires, but we couldn't see it past the lush greenery that surrounded the bungalow. At that moment, I knew we had stepped through the looking glass. Danger and glamour have always coexisted in Hollywood; I just never expected to experience this quite so clearly.

The drive to the airport on Friday was nerve-wracking, to say the least, but I never wondered again if it would be a good idea to move here. I figured any place that could matter-of-factly offer me such weird, surreal experiences was a place where I would be completely at home.

Los Angeles is an easy city to hate. Ask anybody. It's a crowded, smoggy urban sprawl, they say, in which every kind of excess, aberration, and unpleasantness is as close as the next street corner. Everyone who lives here complains about it and longs to get away, back to some place where there's integrity, intellectual stimulation, fresh air, sincere people.

I, on the other hand, dreamed my whole life of coming here. I've lived all over the country in cities and small towns that range from vibrant to beautiful to tedious to annoying. But every time I came out to Los Angeles, I felt instantly at home. I'm excited by the city, fascinated. I don't like the smog or the freeways or the vapid (anything)/actors who populate the place any more than anyone else does. Yet, hardly a day goes by that I don't think about how glad I am to live here. I think one reason for this is that I bring something to Los Angeles that perhaps not everyone does: I can see things that aren't there.

Actually, that sounds like a real California thing to say. But I don't mean it in the Shirley-MacLaine-Psychic-Friends-Network sense. I mean that, for me, the past and present live together in Los Angeles—but not in the same way as in Boston, for instance, or San Antonio or New Orleans. Los Angeles has always been an ultra-modern city that can't wait to obliterate every trace of its own history. But that history is still there, if you know where—and how—to look.

There is an unexceptional little neighborhood down at the east end of Sunset Boulevard. Quiet and plain, there is nothing about it that would rate a tourist's second glance. But I never drive past it without thinking of the

*Intolerence* set

massive Babylon sets—among the largest ever built—which director D.W. Griffith constructed here in 1916 for his epic film *Intolerance*.

On wooded, winding Laurel Canyon Boulevard, an ornate stone stairway leads up the hill to...nothing. But once, years ago, on top of that hill stood the mansion of magician Harry Houdini. The house is gone now, and nothing has ever been built to replace it. Legend has it that Houdini's ghost still walks among those spectral halls. It may be true; *something* lends the place an atmosphere of eerie dread.

Over in Glendale, on Hyperion Street, is the site of the original Walt Disney Studio, where *Steamboat Willie*, the first sound Mickey Mouse cartoon, was produced in 1928, and where *Snow White and the Seven Dwarfs* (1937) and *Pinocchio* (1940) were filmed. Today it is only a strip mall anchored by a supermarket, with little to suggest its illustrious history to the casual visitor. But it's hallowed ground to those of us with a love of animation, present and (particularly) past.

It's the same all over town. The famous Hollywood Canteen, the Garden of Allah apartments, the Hal Roach Studios—all gone, their places taken by parking lots, banks, convenience stores. Other sites, like the original Republic Studios, still stand and are still in business, but unless you know how they are currently being used, you'd never know where to look.

*Los Angeles Uncovered* will show you where to look. It's part guide book, part Los Angeles history, and part celebration of this much maligned—but always intriguing—city. People come here for any number of reasons, and I hope that this book can be of use in any number of ways. Want to create a custom tour of the city? This book will help you find what you want to see. Are you just curious about some landmark you pass all the time? The answer, I hope, is in these pages. Or do you just want to

*Walt Disney Studios in the thirties on Hyperion.*

find those rare pockets of beauty and architectural style in a city that far prefers to be, well, sleek? This book will point you in the right direction.

Students of architecture can locate some of the area's most fascinating buildings.

Movie fans can visit existing movie studios or visit the places where others used to be.

Celebrity hunters can pass the time with history's greatest movie stars in any of the many cemeteries in the area.

And the terminally morbid can drink in the atmosphere at the sites of some of Los Angeles' most gruesome murders and suicides, try to unravel the city's unsolved mysteries, or visit haunted ground where Hollywood's ghosts are said to walk.

*Los Angeles Uncovered* also holds the answers to questions you might never have gotten around to asking. You drive on Wilshire Boulevard every day. You gaze at the Valley below from the winding heights of Mulholland Drive. You have a relaxing picnic out at Griffith Park. Maybe you never gave a second thought to the people who gave their names to these places. But they're in this book, too: heroes, scoundrels, lunatics, killers, thieves—and a few movie producers who were combinations of all of the above.

I hope you'll find *Los Angeles Uncovered* interesting and entertaining to read. But more importantly, I hope it will inspire you to go out and take a closer look at things and places that you've always taken for granted; there are probably more fascinating things in unpromising areas in Los Angeles than in any other city in the world.

And after you've taken that closer look at the wonderful variety of people and places and oddities that make up this city, maybe *Los Angeles Uncovered* can help you take that next step: to see things that aren't there.

# Chapter 1

# The Movie Studios:
# Then and Now

## Lasky Barn and Hollywood's First Movie Studios

In the first decade of this century, if you wanted to make movies, you went where the stars were, where the beautiful locations were, where all of the motion picture technicians, cameramen, editors, writers, and directors were. You went to Fort Lee, New Jersey. For moving pictures, Fort Lee had everything: scenery, access to Broadway actors (and would-be actors), and a bustling community of dedicated movie makers. But there was one real negative to this cinematic Eden...

Weather. Fort Lee had altogether too much of it. Long winters of rain, sleet, and snow were fine if you were making a picture about Eskimos, but even the relatively simpler audiences of 1908 would stand for only so many Frozen North movies and no more.

The answer was simple and effective. The studios established "winter headquarters" in sunnier climes around the country. This practice offered a change of scenery not only to audiences, but to the movie makers themselves. As winter approached each year, companies would head for all points south and west: Florida, Texas, Colorado, and, in increasing numbers, California.

Some movie companies migrated west for another, more compelling, reason: self-preservation. A group of powerful motion picture manufacturers had joined together to form the Motion Picture Patents Company, informally known as the "Trust," to share patents and to try and keep "outsiders" at bay. Independent producers' films were considered "unlicensed," and their use of Trust-patented camera parts could place them in physical danger: the Trust regularly hired thugs to rough up independents, smash their cameras, and confiscate their film. Some independent companies were even fired upon.

Independent producers had to think of ever more elaborate schemes to complete their films in peace (and in one piece). Heading for California—far from the East Coast base of the Trust—was one logical step.

By 1910 the Biograph, Selig, Essanay, Kalem, Lubin, and Pathé companies had sent troupes to Los Angeles. The Centaur Film Company settled there for good in 1911; their Nestor Studio was the first in Hollywood, located at 6101 Sunset Boulevard, on forty acres at the corner of Sunset and Gower.

Just across the street, a year later, the Universal Film Manufacturing Company set up its West Coast headquarters. Universal president Carl Laemmle felt cramped there in the middle of Hollywood, though, and almost immediately began planning a much more expansive (and expensive) place to make more expensive (and expansive) movies. He found the location just over the hill in the San Fernando Valley. He called his new studio Universal City. It's still there today, at the corner of Ventura Boulevard and Lankershim Avenue.

In 1913 the Jesse L. Lasky Feature Play Company secured the rights to the Broadway hit *The Squaw Man* by Edwin Milton Royal and gave director Cecil B. De Mille the job of bringing it to the screen. Reasoning that, "An Indian picture ought to be made in real Indian country," De Mille, star Dustin Farnum, and a few members of the crew set out by train for Flagstaff, Arizona.

Two weeks passed and Lasky heard nothing from De Mille until a cable arrived—from Los Angeles. The director had found Flagstaff completely unsuited to the needs of *The Squaw Man* and had decided to proceed, without permission from the front office, on to Hollywood. There he found a spacious barn at 1520 Vine Street at Selma which he rented for $75 a month to use as a makeshift studio.

Although Lasky was outraged that De Mille had changed plans without consulting the boss, he eventually relented, advising De Mille to rent on a month-to-month basis. Soon, the property became the West Coast branch of the Lasky company and, ultimately, the home of Paramount Pictures [see below]. The company moved to studios on Melrose and Van Ness Avenue in 1926, and the following year the original studio was razed to make room for a miniature golf course. The barn, however, was spared. It was moved over to the Paramount Studio where it stayed until the late 1970s, when it was moved to a location at 2100 Highland, just across from the Hollywood Bowl.

Today the old barn, now called the Hollywood Studio Museum, is open for tours. Once a month the Silent Society, a group dedicated to silent movies, sponsors screenings of early films, which are open to the public.

In 1915 William H. Clune, an exhibitor, decided to start making movies instead of merely showing them. He bought a studio from Fiction Pictures at 650 North Bronson at Melrose Avenue and produced an acclaimed version of the classic story *Ramona* (1917). Later, Douglas Fairbanks' production company leased the Clune

Studios to make his wildly popular *The Three Musketeers* (1921). It was known as the California Studios in the thirties, the Producers Studios in the fifties and sixties, and was renamed the Raleigh Studios in 1980. The studio remains a busy spot for both feature film and television production.

## The Mack Sennett Studios

1712 Glendale, Glendale

*Mack Sennett Studios—1916*

Although considered just another part of Los Angeles now, when Mack Sennett made his frenetic Keystone Cop movies here between 1912 and 1928, this area bore the more euphonious name of Edendale. Contemporary photographs show that the name wasn't far wrong; California was a kind of Eden in those days. The sun was always shining, the air was filled with the luxurious scent of orange blossoms, and you never knew when a Sennett Bathing Beauty might come strolling into view.

It has been claimed that the very first pie ever thrown in a movie was thrown at this studio in 1913. The tosser was Mabel Normand; the recipient, Roscoe "Fatty" Arbuckle. This may or may not be true, but it is inarguable that many a pie would eventually be thrown in this place called the Laugh Factory. The largest of the original stages still stands; today, it is a commercial storage space.

# D.W. Griffith Studios

4400-4500 Sunset, Hollywood

In late 1915 the residents of this quiet little neighborhood were slightly alarmed to notice that a movie set was being constructed in their backyards. A big movie set—the biggest set ever built in Hollywood, even to this day. Cinema pioneer D.W. Griffith was recreating ancient Babylon for his epic *Intolerance* (1916). To the residents, in retrospect, having this huge ancient city tower over their homes for the time it took to produce the movie was

*D.W. Griffith*

5

probably the good part. The bad part was that the *Intolerance* set just sat there for years, slowly rotting away.

Across Sunset Boulevard were the Griffith Studios where most of his major productions of the teens were produced and where gifted actors like Lillian and Dorothy Gish, Robert Harron, Donald Crisp, Mae Marsh, and Henry Walthall became famous movie stars.

Today, absolutely nothing remains of the Griffith Studios. The site is filled with strip malls and parking lots. Ironically, several neighboring houses, plainly identifiable from the 1915-1916 period, still stand, relatively unchanged.

# Charlie Chaplin Studios

1416 La Brea, Hollywood

By 1918 Charlie Chaplin was the most popular movie star in the world. He had just signed a contract with First National Films to produce eight two-reel pictures for a fee of more than a million dollars. After having worked at such studios as Essanay, Keystone, and Mutual, Chaplin was ready to build his own. This he did on a rural stretch of La Brea Avenue, designing the studio to resemble a cozy Swiss village.

In 1966, over a decade after Chaplin had been exiled to, oddly enough, a cozy (well, lavish) Swiss estate, the studio was purchased by musician Herb Alpert as headquarters for his record label, A&M Records. Clearly visible from the street, the studio has remained remarkably similar to its original appearance of nearly eight decades ago.

*Charlie Chaplin Studios, Los Angeles, California*

# Buster Keaton Studios

1025 Lillian Way, Hollywood

Chaplin made some of his excellent Mutual Films at this studio near the intersection of Vine Street and Santa Monica Boulevard in 1916, but it became Buster Keaton Studios in 1920. Beginning with *The High Sign* (1920), all of Keaton's films were made here (or using it as a home base) until 1928 and his last independent production *Steamboat Bill, Jr.* Today an equipment rental business occupies the property. There are a few random buildings that date back to Keaton's day, but, by and large, there is nothing to indicate that this site was once the home of some of film history's most brilliant comedies.

# The Goldwyn Studios

(a.k.a. Warner Hollywood)
1041 Formosa, Hollywood

There are two ways in which movie mogul Sam Goldwyn has stuck in the popular memory. One is as the producer of some of the most literate, sensitive, and memorable classics of the screen: *Dodsworth* (1936), *Wuthering Heights* (1939), *The Pride of the Yankees* (1942), *The Best Years of Our Lives* (1946).

The other is as the origin of some of the greatest malaprops ever to spring from Hollywood: "A verbal contract isn't worth the paper it's written on"; "Include me out!"; "Anyone seeing a psychiatrist should have his head examined"; and the immortal, "I don't care if it makes a nickel! I just want every man, woman, and child in America to see it!"

This studio was built in 1920. Mary Pickford and Douglas Fairbanks had been running it since 1922, and when Goldwyn became their partner five years later, he renamed it The Goldwyn Studios.

Throughout the thirties and forties, many wonderful films were made on this site: Eddie Cantor's musical comedies—featuring that bevy of babes, the Goldwyn Girls—like *Whoopee* (1930) and *Kid Millions* (1935); Ronald Colman vehicles such as *Arrowsmith* (1931) and *Cynara* (1932); and masterworks by distinguished directors like Howard Hawks, King Vidor, and William Wyler. Gary Cooper made *The Real Glory* (1939) and *The Westerner* (1940)—among others—at Goldwyn. Danny Kaye made most of his classic comedies here, including *The Secret Life of Walter Mitty* (1947) and *Hans Christian Andersen* (1952). Bob Hope starred in *The Princess and the Pirate* (1946). And, on this lot, Cary Grant, David

Niven, and Loretta Young appeared in the Christmas perennial *The Bishop's Wife* (1947).

Warner Bros. took over the property after Goldwyn retired in the early sixties, and the studio today is known as Warner Hollywood. In some ways it is the least changed of the major studio lots. Its buildings are comfortably old-fashioned, the stairways steep and narrow, the elevators built for two, the soundstages dark and musty. At the right time of day it isn't hard to imagine that Danny Kaye might come strolling out of one of them, in costume for *Up In Arms*, or that you might catch Eddie Cantor joking around with a gang of the Goldwyn Girls. And if you listen closely, you might hear Cathy's plaintive calls for Heathcliff, across the moors of *Wuthering Heights*. Or maybe it's just a construction crew, a couple of blocks down Formosa....

# Metro-Goldwyn-Mayer

(now Sony Pictures; see Columbia Studios)
10202 Washington Blvd., Culver City

There are still clues to the past around this sprawling lot but little to suggest that this was once the site of one of Hollywood's biggest, most important and impressive studios, the company that boasted "more stars than there are in Heaven." For over half a century, while M-G-M maintained ownership of the property, this was the site of countless great films, from *Ben-Hur* (1925) to *Mutiny on the Bounty* (1935) to *Singin' in the Rain* (1952) to, well, *Ben-Hur* (1959). By the mid-thirties, M-G-M had twenty-three soundstages and over 100 acres of backlot sets which included a lake and harbor, a park, a jungle, city streets, suburban neighborhoods (like where Andy Hardy lived), and European villages. By the mid-seventies, most of it was gone: props (like Dorothy's ruby slippers from *The Wizard of Oz*) were sold at auction; sets were torn down and property sold off.

Today, the massive white Irving Thalberg Building, named after the studio's beloved production head who died in 1936, is a symbol of the glory that was M-G-M. But, of course, today the place is no longer M-G-M.

Metro Pictures was formed in 1915. Throughout the teens, the studio produced its pictures (like Rudolph Valentino's *The Four Horsemen of the Apocalypse* (1921)) at facilities at 6300 Romaine in Hollywood. Buster Keaton released his masterworks through Metro, and little Jackie Coogan was the studio's biggest star. No trace of that studio remains on Romaine today.

*M-G-M's original gate—still there on Washington Ave. in Culver City*

Metro merged with Goldwyn Pictures and producer Louis B. Mayer in 1924 to form Metro-Goldwyn-Mayer (Sam Goldwyn, by the way, was no longer connected with the studio with which he shared a name). The new corporation took over Triangle Studios, a facility in Culver City which had been built in 1915 by Thomas Ince, Mack Sennett, and D.W. Griffith. The original Triangle main gate, a long white-pillared structure, still stands along Washington Boulevard, although it is no longer in use.

Many of the soundstages built in the thirties still stand, as do some of the original dressing rooms and other facilities, but the site only barely resembles the movie factory it was during its incredible heyday. Over the years M-G-M has been bought and sold more than once, merging with United Artists, being acquired then quickly disposed of by Ted Turner. Today, the lot is owned by Sony Pictures (which, in turn, owns Columbia Pictures). There is a striking irony here. In the old days, M-G-M was the cream of Hollywood, while Columbia was known primarily as a low-budget pretender. Today, the walls of the Thalberg Building are lined with the posters of films that Irving Thalberg himself would have dismissed with a contemptuous sniff. *Sic Semper* Hollywood.

# Paramount Pictures

5451 Marathon, Hollywood

Its ornate studio gate has been a symbol of the Hollywood system for decades. Of course, while it's still there, the gate isn't in use anymore, and that's kind of a symbol, too.

Indisputably the biggest, most important movie studio in the twenties, Paramount has maintained its prominence in all the decades since. From the beginning, the studio produced well-crafted, immensely popular films like James Cruze's *The Covered Wagon* and Cecil B. De Mille's *The Ten Commandments* (both 1923). Throughout the twenties, Paramount maintained two busy studios, one in Hollywood and one in Astoria, Long Island, New York.

Paramount moved into the Marathon Street location in 1926 and began making prestigious films like *Beau Geste* (1926) and *Wings* (1927; the first film to win the Academy Award for Best Production). Harold Lloyd released his powerfully popular films through Paramount, while Clara Bow was the studio's biggest star. Paramount in the twenties was home to W.C. Fields, William Powell, Pola Negri, Louise Brooks, and the phenomenally popular (though, sadly, almost forgotten) Nancy Carroll.

In the thirties, Paramount made movie stars of the Marx Brothers (who made most of their films at Astoria), Maurice Chevalier, Fredric March, Jeannette MacDonald, Gary Cooper, Mae West, and Marlene Dietrich, among many others. Bob Hope and Bing Crosby started out at Paramount in the thirties and were the studio's biggest stars by the early forties with their hilarious *Road* pictures. Betty Hutton made her films on this site. So did Barbara Stanwyck, the great writer-director Preston Sturges, Alan Ladd, and Veronica Lake.

So many classic films were made at Paramount during that rich period, in fact, that it seems futile to even try to suggest the studio's variety and quality: *Beau Geste* (1939), *The Lady Eve* (1942), *This Gun For Hire* (1942), *Holiday Inn* (1942), *Double Indemnity* (1944), *The Lost Weekend* (1945), *The Paleface* (1948), *Sunset Boulevard* (1950), and hundreds of others.

Paramount's biggest stars in the fifties were Dean Martin and Jerry Lewis. When the team broke up and

*Paramount in 1950*

Lewis began directing his own films, he set *The Errand Boy* (1961) on the Paramount lot. Although he renamed the studio "Paramutual" for the film, *The Errand Boy* is a priceless look behind the scenes. Other films that use the Paramount studio itself as a setting include *Star Spangled Rhythm* (1942), *Variety Girl* (1947), and *Sunset Boulevard*.

To combat 20th Century-Fox's widescreen format CinemaScope, Paramount developed a system called VistaVision which, with its larger negative, produced better visual clarity and substantially better sound fidelity. The first VistaVision release was *White Christmas* (1954), starring Bing Crosby, Danny Kaye, Rosemary Clooney, and Vera Ellen. It was followed by other blockbusters, produced on this site, like Cecil B. De Mille's *The Ten*

*Commandments*, Alfred Hitchcock's *The Man Who Knew Too Much*, and *The Court Jester* (all 1956), starring Danny Kaye.

Today, Paramount divides its space between feature films and television productions. Getting a tour of the studio itself isn't so easy, but getting into some of the old stages certainly is: tickets for tapings of sitcoms such as *Married With Children* are free.

# RKO

780 Gower, Hollywood

These days it's difficult to tell where Paramount stops and RKO starts; it's all one big happy studio now. But if you look up to the top of the outer walls, you can still see the globe that was once RKO's logo.

RKO, at the corner of Gower and Marathon, started life as Robertson-Cole Studios in 1920. It became Film Booking Offices of America, Inc. (FBO) two years later. Joseph Kennedy bought the company in 1926 and began producing low-budget pictures, mostly Westerns, starring Bob Steele and Tom Mix.

When David Sarnoff, president of RCA, decided to get in on the ground floor of that new phenomenon, talking pictures, he bought a large interest in FBO. The company struggled for a while until FBO acquired a chain of theaters—the Keith-Albee-Orpheum circuit of vaudeville houses—through which it could release its films. In 1928 FBO's name was changed to Radio-Keith-Orpheum Corporation or RKO. From 1928 to 1931 RKO produced its films mainly in Culver City [see Selznick Studios]. The studio also owned a 500-acre ranch in Encino where Westerns and other outdoor films were shot.

In its first years, RKO was not known for the quality of its output. With the exception of films like *A Bill of Divorcement* (1932), in which Katharine Hepburn made her movie debut, and *The Most Dangerous Game* (1932), starring Fay Wray and Joel McCrea, the studio's motion pictures tended to be rather dull and unexciting. The teaming of Fred Astaire and Ginger Rogers in 1933 changed all that. In no time, RKO was producing some of the best films in Hollywood: *King Kong* (1933), *Little Women* (1933), *Of Human Bondage* (1934), *The Informer* (1935), *Stage Door* (1937), *Bringing Up Baby* (1938), and *The Hunchback of Notre Dame* (1939).

*RKO Radio Pictures 1940. Globe is still there, corner of Gower and Melrose.*

In 1941 RKO produced what many still feel is the best motion picture ever made: Orson Welles' *Citizen Kane*. Producer Val Lewton made a series of intelligent, literate, and frightening horror films with lurid titles like *I Walked With a Zombie* (1944) and *The Body Snatcher* (1945); the Lewton films also gave the start to a few famous film directors like Robert Wise, Jacques Tourneur, and Mark Robson.

In 1948 Howard Hughes bought the studio, and many of its most talented citizens jumped ship rather than work with the eccentric billionaire. Hughes eventually sold out at an enormous profit, and in 1957 RKO was purchased by Desilu, the company owned by Desi Arnaz and Lucille Ball. Ironically, Lucille Ball had started out as a bit player at the studio two decades earlier before becoming powerful enough through her television series *I Love Lucy* to buy the joint herself. The ultimate Hollywood revenge.

## Universal

3900 Lankershim Blvd., Universal City

"Uncle" Carl Laemmle, the head of Universal Pictures, originally established his studio near all the other studios in downtown Hollywood. But Uncle Carl's dreams needed more elbow room, so he found a remote piece of land, just over the Hollywood Hills in the San Fernando Valley, and started creating a 230-acre empire. Laemmle opened the doors to Universal City on March 15, 1915; one of the guests on that gala day was Buffalo Bill Cody.

Universal was one of the major forces of the American cinema during the silent era. Lon Chaney made *The Hunchback of Notre Dame* (1923) and *Phantom of the*

*Opera* (1925) here, and Erich von Stroheim directed such celebrated epics as *Foolish Wives* (1922) and *The Merry-Go-Round* (1923). Rudolph Valentino made films here; so did such celebrated stars as Mae Murray, Reginald Denney, and Harry Carey.

Horror movie fans revere Universal as the home of some of the enduring classics of the genre: *Frankenstein* (1931), with Boris Karloff; *Dracula* (1931), starring Bela Lugosi; *The Invisible Man* (1935), with Claude Rains; *The Wolf Man* (1941) starring Lon Chaney Jr.; and Alfred Hitchcock's *Psycho* (1960).

The Depression hit Universal hard, but a bright little singer named Deanna Durbin kept the studio afloat

*Universal Studios—1936*

during the thirties. In the forties, Abbott and Costello were the studio's leading lights, and Universal was best known for its low-budget B-pictures and series films, like the Francis series, starring Donald O'Connor and a talking mule.

More recently, Universal is the place where Steven Spielberg got his start, making such films as *The Sugarland Express* (1974) and *Jaws* (1975) for the studio—not to mention a popular little tidbit called *E.T.: The Extra-Terrestrial* (1982).

Laemmle offered tours of the studio from the very beginning, charging 25 cents a head, which included a box lunch. The tours stopped when sound movies came in, because of the sensitive recording equipment. But Universal started them again in 1964. Little by little the tour became more elaborate, with many attractions, shows, rides, restaurants, and theaters.

Today the Universal Tour is a full-fledged theme park. The tourist can have a great time but will probably not see any actual filming in progress. Riding on a tram, you can get snapped at by Jaws, grabbed at by King Kong, drenched by a sudden flash flood, and shaken by an earthquake (or, this being California, maybe two).

In the early nineties, Universal opened the City Walk, an idealized Los Angeles neighborhood offering all the shopping, sight-seeing, and fine restaurants of, say, Hollywood Boulevard, with less threat of actual violence and bloodshed.

# Selznick International

9336 Washington Blvd., Culver City

Before the credits of *Gone With the Wind* (1939) begin, we see a white sign, swinging from two chains, bearing the legend: "A Selznick International Picture." Behind the sign is a huge, white mansion that looks like the home of the most prosperous plantation owner in the South. In fact, it is a replica of George Washington's home, Mount Vernon, built in 1924 as a set for Thomas Ince's *Barbara Freitchie*. Cecil B. De Mille converted the building into office space when he took over the studio in 1925. The mansion is still there today, easily visible from Washington Boulevard. It fronts a small movie lot

*Selznick International—1930s*

known as the Culver Studios, but to moviegoers it will always signify the opulent cinema of David O. Selznick. In addition to *Gone With the Wind*, such classic Selznick films as *A Star Is Born* (1937) and *Nothing Sacred* (1937)—and many others—were filmed on this lot.

Ince built the studio in 1918, and after Pathé and De Mille (he made the silent 1927 version of *The King of Kings* at this studio) ran the place for a while, RKO took it over. The Astaire/Rogers musicals such as *The Gay Divorcee* (1934) and *Top Hat* (1935) were filmed on this lot, as was the biggest monkey movie of them all, *King Kong* (1933).

Today the studio and its fourteen sound stages are owned by Sony Pictures, which also owns the former M-G-M Studio just down the street.

# Hal Roach

8822 Washington Blvd., Culver City

Only a plaque marks the location of what was once the source of more laughter than any other studio in Hollywood. The classic Our Gang comedies were produced at this location, as were most of the great comedies by our dear friends Mr. Laurel and Mr. Hardy. Although the studio is gone, torn down in the late fifties, fans of the Roach comedies will notice many locations from those films nearby; many a frantic car chase took place on Washington Boulevard and the surrounding streets.

[For a highly entertaining guide to these Laurel and Hardy and Our Gang locations, see *Following the Comedy Trail* by Leon Smith, Los Angeles: Pomegranate Press, Ltd., 1988.]

*Hal E. Roach Studios*

## Columbia

1438 Gower, Hollywood

On a still night, if you listen closely, you may still be able to hear a "Nyuk Nyuk Nyuk" or a "Paging Dr. Howard, Dr. Fine, Dr. Howard" floating in the breeze. It was at this location, once known as Poverty Row, that the Three Stooges tossed pies and poked eyes, reason enough, in my mind, for the still-standing soundstages to be treated with a kind of hushed reverence.

Columbia head Harry Cohn built Columbia Studios on this site in 1921. Columbia was the least of the majors until director Frank Capra came along and made a name (and a fortune and several Academy Awards) for himself and the studio. Capra's classics *It Happened One Night* (1934), *Mr. Deeds Goes to Town* (1936), and *You Can't Take it With You* (1938) were filmed right here.

In 1972 Columbia began sharing the Warner Bros. Studios in Burbank [see Warner Bros. below], thus changing the name to the Burbank Studios. In 1989, after Columbia Pictures was purchased by the Sony Corporation, the company moved again, to the former M-G-M Studios in Culver City [see M-G-M above].

# Republic

4024 Radford Ave., Studio City

*Republic Studios in 1956*

Today, it is known as CBS Studio Center where hit television shows such as *Seinfeld* and *The Larry Sanders Show* are produced. But decades ago it was Cowboy Heaven, home to John Wayne, Roy Rogers, Gene Autrey, Bob Steele and so many other sagebrush heroes.

Republic produced B-pictures almost exclusively but somehow did the job better than any of the other low-budget studios like Monogram or PRC. Occasionally, the studio backed a bigger-budget film like John Ford's *The Quiet Man* (1952) or the epic of the Alamo *The Last Command* (1955), but by the late fifties, Republic had virtually abandoned motion pictures and adopted the medium in which low budgets and shoddy production values were the norm: television.

## Monogram

4376 Sunset, Hollywood

Another Poverty Row studio, Monogram produced movies that were, if not actually the bottom of the barrel, only a slat or two away. Built in 1912 by Sigmund Lubin, the studio was owned at various times by such diverse companies as Kalem (1913), Allied Artists (1952), and Colorvision TV (1967).

The East Side Kids (a.k.a. The Dead End Kids, The Bowery Boys, etc.) made movies at Monogram between 1940 and 1950, and series pictures like the Charlie Chan movies were produced here, too. The lot has been owned since 1970 by KCET-TV, a public broadcasting station. A few of the Monogram buildings still stand at the site, and you can actually feel your standards dropping as you get closer to them.

# Walt Disney Studios

When the young animator moved to California from his native Chicago in 1923, he moved in with his uncle Robert Disney at 4606 Kingswell. Walt created some of his first cartoons in the garage out back. In 1925 Walt and his brother Roy opened a small animation studio down the street in a storefront at 4649 Kingswell. This building still stands and is today occupied by a printing shop.

A year later, the Disneys moved to a more professional studio at 2719 Hyperion in Glendale. For the next decade, they made landmark animated films here: the first sound cartoon, *Steamboat Willie* (1927; it was also the first Mickey Mouse cartoon released, although it was the third produced); the first three-strip Technicolor cartoon, *Flowers and Trees* (1932), and the studio's first feature-length cartoon, *Snow White and the Seven Dwarfs* (1937). Today, the site is only a parking lot. Up the street is a building marked Hyperion Studios, but it has no connection to Disney history.

In 1940 Disney expanded his operations by moving into a brand new studio in Burbank at 500 South Buena Vista. The studio is still there today, although several grotesque new buildings have spoiled the art deco charm of the original. At this studio, all of the animated features from *Fantasia* (1940) on were produced. Disney's television productions like *The Mickey Mouse Club* and *Disneyland* were filmed here, as were the live action adventures, fantasies, and comedies that enthralled several generations: *Davy Crockett, King of the Wild Frontier* (1955), *Darby O'Gill and the Little People* (1959), *The Shaggy Dog* (1959), *Pollyanna* (1960), *The Parent Trap* (1961).

More recently, such blockbuster hits as *Beauty and the Beast* (1990), *Aladdin* (1992), and *The Lion King* (1994) were created primarily at this studio.

Today, many television series are videotaped on the Disney lot. It is with a certain amount of irony that one notes the fact that the hit ABC series *Home Improvement*, starring Tim Allen, is shot on the same stage that once housed the Great Hall of the Leprechauns' King Brian in *Darby O'Gill and the Little People*; or that *Ellen*, starring Ellen Degeneres, is videotaped on a stage where Captain Nemo fought a death struggle with a giant squid in *20,000 Leagues Under the Sea* (1954). As *Sunset Boulevard's* Norma Desmond would say, "It's the pictures that got small...."

# 20th Century-Fox

10201 W. Pico Boulevard, Century City

The 20th Century-Fox backlot used to spread over hundreds of acres of what is now Century City. Today there isn't much left, although as you drive by on Pico Boulevard you can still catch a glimpse of the massive "New York Street" built for Gene Kelly's *Hello, Dolly!* (1969) and used in many subsequent movies.

When William Fox founded Fox Film Corporation in 1915, he soon built his first studio at 1417-18 N. Western Avenue in Hollywood. It was here that Theda Bara made such epics as *Cleopatra* (1917), where William Farnum and Tom Mix rode the range, and where John Wayne made his first screen appearance in 1928. Janet Gaynor and Charles Farrell were two of Fox's biggest stars of the twenties, and such screen classics as F.W. Murnau's

*Sunrise* (1927) and John Ford's *The Iron Horse* (1924) were made at this studio. Will Rogers made virtually all the films here that earned him the position of top box-office draw of the early thirties.

In 1935 Fox merged with Twentieth Century, a company owned by Darryl F. Zanuck and Joseph M. Schenck. The resulting corporation, 20th Century-Fox, turned out countless great (and profitable) films in the thirties and forties, including *Young Mr. Lincoln* (1939), *In Old Chicago* (1939), *How Green Was My Valley* (1941), *The Ox-Bow Incident* (1943), and the films of Shirley Temple, Alice Faye, Betty Grable, and many others.

In 1953, 20th Century-Fox changed the face of movies by introducing their new anamorphic widescreen process CinemaScope. Beginning with *The Robe* (1953) and *How to Marry a Millionaire* (1953), every Fox film was released in CinemaScope until the late sixties. All of the other studios had to follow suit, resulting in a decade of experimentation with a diverse, often bewildering array of new screen shapes and sizes: Cinerama, 3-D, Panavision, VistaVision, Todd-AO, and many, many others.

In the early sixties, the Fox production *Cleopatra*, starring Elizabeth Taylor and Richard Burton, made headlines around the world when the stars' romance flared on the set (they later divorced their respective spouses and married each other, a couple of times). Unfortunately, the incredible publicity avalanche couldn't bring enough people into theaters to make *Cleopatra* pay off. Estimates of the film's cost range from $40 to $60 million, very high for a film today, but downright astronomical over thirty years ago. It nearly ruined the studio, leading to the ouster of its studio head and the reinstatement of the original boss, Darryl Zanuck, whose son Richard also rose through the ranks to became a Hollywood powerhouse.

20th Century-Fox remains one of Hollywood's busiest and most successful studios and is still pretty impressive to see, if you don't happen to remember what a giant cinematic wonderland it was a half century ago.

# Warner Bros.

4000 Warner Blvd., Burbank

When I was a kid, my favorite television shows nearly all came from the same studio: Warner Bros. In the moments before the credits (and wonderful theme songs) of *Cheyenne*, *77 Sunset Strip*, *Hawaiian Eye*, or *Sugar Foot*, there would come on the screen an aerial shot of the studios in Burbank. It looked like a sea of hangar-like soundstages; the image defined "moviemaking" to me. I never walk among those soundstages today without thinking of that kid in South Carolina, dreaming of Hollywood. And, to this day, the Warners lot continues to define "moviemaking" to me.

Like those of the other major studios, the story of Warner Bros.'s path to this studio is a fairly complex one. Sam, Jack L., Harry, and Albert Warner were nickelodeon operators in Pennsylvania around the turn of the century who eventually turned their entrepreneurial talents to producing and distributing films. They came out to California in 1917 and established headquarters in Hollywood at 5858 Sunset (now KCET-TV Channel 5) in 1919. In 1925 they expanded their operations by purchasing the old Vitagraph Studios in Hollywood at 4151 Prospect.

By this time, Warner Bros. had become fascinated with the idea of sound films and decided to experiment with a sound-on-disc system. They filmed *Don Juan*, starring John Barrymore and Mary Astor, at the Warner Bros.-Vitagraph Studios in 1926 and released it with a recorded soundtrack of music and sound effects. Over the next year they filmed over one hundred Vitaphone shorts, both in Hollywood and in New York.

Their biggest success with sound—and the movie that has erroneously become known as the first talkie—was *The Jazz Singer*, starring Al Jolson, which was released in 1927. *The Jazz Singer* was filmed at the Sunset studio.

Another company, First National Films, began making movies at 4000 Warner Boulevard in Burbank in 1926, about the time the Warners began to realize the first fruits of their success. Three years later, in 1929, Warner Bros. took over First National and moved the base of operations to Burbank. However, both the Sunset and Prospect studios remained in use for years. Many films, such as *Little Caesar* (1930) or *Golddiggers of 1933* (1933), were shot at two, or even all three, of the studios.

It was in this expansive Burbank studio that most of the great Warner Bros. films were made: *The Public Enemy* (1931), *42nd Street* (1933), *The Adventures of Robin Hood* (1938), *Dark Victory* (1939), *Casablanca* (1943); the films of Bette Davis, Humphrey Bogart, James Cagney, Ronald Reagan, Ann Sheridan, Errol Flynn, and Olivia de Havilland.

The Warner Bros. animation department, affectionately known by the animators as "Termite Terrace," remained at 5858 Sunset Boulevard until the mid-fifties. In terms of sheer star power, it's hard to beat the personalities that came out of Termite Terrace: it's the birthplace of Bugs Bunny, Daffy Duck, Elmer Fudd, Porky Pig, Foghorn Leghorn, Tweetie-Pie, Sylvester the Cat, Yosemite Sam, Pepe le Pew, the Road Runner, Wile E. Coyote and so many others.

Warner Bros. boasts the tallest soundstage in the country, Stage 16, raised some fifteen feet by William

Randolph Hearst to accommodate a scene in *Cain and Mabel* (1935), a musical starring Clark Gable and Hearst's mistress Marion Davies. More recently, Stage 16 served as the set for the giant three-story cryo-prison in *Demolition Man* (1993).

Warner Bros. is the only major studio which offers a tour. Not a faked-up tour like the one at Universal City, but a real walk through the soundstages, sets, and technical departments of a major studio. The V.I.P. Tour is highly recommended for anyone with a serious interest in filmmaking. And also for anyone who spent their childhoods gazing wistfully at that magical expanse of soundstages called Warner Bros. Studios.

For information regarding the V.I.P Tour call (818) 954-1744.

*Warner Bros at 5858 Sunset in the early twenties. Now the site of KCET-TV.*

# Chapter II

# L.A. Ghost Stories

When we think of classic ghost stories we think of ancient mansions with moonlit hallways and cobweb-covered staircases. We think of howling winds, crashing thunder, the clank...clank...clank of spectral chains dragging across the floor, and the unearthly wail of a damned soul.

Well, there aren't any ancient mansions in Los Angeles, unless you call 1902 ancient. Not much crashing thunder, either. But we do have howling Santa Ana winds, and if you want to hear the unearthly wail of damned souls, just go to Hollywood Boulevard at about 3 a.m.

But ghosts do walk in Los Angeles. This town perhaps doesn't have the longest of histories. But there are those who say that human misery can keep a spirit chained to its earthly home; and of that, L.A. has all it needs.

The following ghost stories have been gathered from several sources. One of them—*Hollywood Haunted* by Laurie Jacobson and Marc Wanamaker—was published just as I wrapped up the writing of this book, and I enthusiastically recommend it if this kind of spooky tale is up your alley. See the bibliography at the end for particulars.

Otherwise, you can enjoy these yarns in one of several ways: as just good, creepy stories; as fractured variations on Hollywood history and legend; or, since I provide addresses (where possible), as the basis for your own Hollywood Ghost Tour.

If you do actually visit these sites, please don't disturb the inhabitants—living *or* dead....

## The *Queen Mary*

Port of Long Beach

The 81,237-ton *Queen Mary* was the biggest passenger liner ever to sail the seas. She is 1,019 feet long, twelve decks high, and contains over 1,000 portholes and windows. Since 1964 she has rested in permanent dry dock in Long Beach and has now been turned into a hotel/shopping mall. The old ship has been restored and is both beautiful and impressive. In the movies it has stood in for both the *Poseidon* (*The Poseidon Adventure*, 1972) and the *Titanic* (*S.O.S. Titanic*, 1979).

In some parts of the ship, it's easy to imagine yourself as a privileged passenger of fifty years ago. But the past that lives aboard the *Queen Mary* is comprised of more than furnishing and fittings. There are those who insist that people—or at least their spirits—from the past are still very much in evidence.

Many workers on the ship have heard unexplained noises, most commonly a clanging sound as though from someone banging on pipes with a hammer. A security officer briefly saw a woman in a forties-era bathing suit about to dive into the empty swimming pool—the woman disappeared instantly. A tour guide was closing an exhibit one day when a man stepped up behind her. As she stepped aside to let him pass he disappeared.

More recently a reporter from a "reality based" television show took video equipment to the swimming pool area and recorded what he claimed was the ghostly voice of a little girl. The ship's records indicate that a woman once drowned in the pool, but otherwise there seems to be no specific explanation as to why that area seems particularly ghostly.

Other *Queen Mary* ghosts include an evening-gowned woman seen in the salon and an officer who frequents the bridge where, it is said, he died of accidental poisoning.

# The Hollywood Roosevelt Hotel

7000 Hollywood Boulevard

Recently (in 1984) renovated to its former beauty, the Hollywood Roosevelt is redolent with history. Among other things, it was the site of the first Academy Awards ceremony in 1929. If you want a crash course in Hollywood history, this is an excellent place to come. Photographs which detail the story of Hollywood line the upper balcony.

Through the years, some of the greatest stars in Hollywood stayed at the Roosevelt. Today, it seems, the ghostly register is just as impressive.

The spirit of Marilyn Monroe is said to linger there; her reflection has been glimpsed in a mirror that once hung in the suite (Number 1200) she often stayed in.

Montgomery Clift may also haunt Room 928, where he lived for three months in 1952. Several people have reported feeling the touch of a hand or catching a glimpse of someone who *might* look like Clift.

And, according to *Hollywood Haunted*, a psychic has felt the "impressions" of Errol Flynn, Betty Grable, Gypsy Rose Lee, Ethel Merman, Humphrey Bogart,

Carmen Miranda, and many other celebrities at various places around the Roosevelt.

## The Houdini Estate

2398 Laurel Canyon

Harry Houdini

Houdini, possibly the world's greatest illusionist, was obsessed with the supernatural. More specifically, he was obsessed with proving that mediums and psychics were frauds and that their seances and spiritualist services were nothing more than well-rehearsed shows for grieving, gullible people.

But he retained an open mind. He told his wife that he would try to contact her after his death with a secret code that only she would know. He died on Halloween, 1926. Every year since, on the anniversary of that date, a seance has been held to contact Houdini, to no avail.

The remains of his estate—arched stone supports and a deteriorating stone stairway—can be seen by passing cars on Laurel Canyon Road. At the top of those stairs stand the servant's quarters, the only buildings remaining. The spot has remained vacant—one might even say desolate—for decades, and reports of odd sounds and strange lights are common. It is generally accepted, especially by those who live nearby, that the Houdini estate is haunted.

But by whom? It appears that, although he owned it, Houdini himself never actually lived here. Besides, if his ghost were to return to earth, would it walk the grounds of some lonely, nearly forgotten estate? Or would it have come back earlier, to contact the woman he loved, using their secret seance code?

## Huntington Hartford Estate

2000 Fuller, Hollywood

This may or may not be a haunted place. I've never read or heard anything to suggest it is. I only know what happened to me when I visited it several years ago.

During a visit to Los Angeles in 1984 (I lived in Atlanta, Georgia at the time) I spent half of my time doing research for a book I was working on and the other half just touring around Hollywood. A friend, who knew of my predilection for ruins, suggested that I visit the Huntington Hartford Estate. I learned from a tour book that it had been built in 1919 and that Irish tenor John McCormick (a particular favorite of mine) had once lived there.

Huntington Hartford, a supermarket magnate, purchased the land in 1942. For reasons known only to himself, Hartford did not take care of the house or grounds, and over a period of decades, everything fell to ruin.

I found the entrance, at the seeming dead end of Fuller, just off Franklin, hopped over the chain that stretched over the drive, and stepped into the past. Only some steps and parts of foundations remained to mark where the mansion once stood. Here were the remains of two tennis courts. Farther along were long-empty swimming pools. I was absolutely fascinated. For reasons I've never quite understood, I've always been more thrilled by ruins than by actual buildings.

But suddenly, and for no reason that I could tell, I was completely drenched with fear. It was still a bright, sunny day, nothing had happened to change the tranquility of the landscape, but I was terrified. I almost began to panic and ran for the estate entrance as fast as I could. The instant I was on the other side of the chain, the fear vanished and I felt more than a little foolish. But did I go back in there? Not on your life.

# Ozzie and Harriet's House

1822 Camino Palermo, Beverly Hills

Bandleader-turned-television producer/director/star Ozzie Nelson had a very simple idea when someone suggested that he create a comedy radio show. He would base the situations on his own life. His wife on the show would be played by his real wife Harriet, his sons by real sons David and Ricky. He even modeled the sets after the real Nelson home in Beverly Hills. Sometimes, the exterior of the house was actually seen in the show. When the show made the transition to television, it was an instant and enduring hit. The Nelsons seemed to be the ideal family: warm, interesting, funny, loving.

Ozzie died of cancer in 1975, and Harriet lived in the house for a few more years before selling it. Ever since, there have been numerous reports that a ghost—possibly that of Ozzie himself—haunts the place.

Subsequent owners have reported that lights go on and off without reason, that water faucets are suddenly turned on by no one visible, and doors open and close by themselves. One woman who lived in the house reported that the ghostly doings are of a more personal nature; she reported that unseen hands caressed her and invisible lips kissed her neck and breasts.

No one has ever been able to determine for sure that this mischievous, randy ghost is actually Ozzie Nelson. If it is, he's not quite the innocent, wholesome fella he used to be.

# Chapter III

# The Names
# Behind the Names

## Griffith Park

In 1896 Colonel Griffith J. Griffith donated 3,500 acres of hilly property to the City of Los Angeles. The land used to be the Rancho Los Feliz, but Griffith thought that it would make a nice city park. It took several decades for Griffith Park to be developed, but eventually it was, and today it has a zoo and a miniature train to ride and lots of horse paths and plenty of parking. If you're there on a Sunday afternoon, lying around on the grass (some distance from the horse path is suggested), enjoying a leisurely picnic and breathing in what passes for fresh air, you might give a thought to Col. Griffith and think that he was probably a swell fella.

Well, think again.

He was, to put it politely, a loon. In 1903 he began to believe that his wife was plotting with the Pope to poison him and overthrow the government. Now, to be fair, we don't know that his wife *wasn't* plotting with the Pope, but even so, Col. Griffith probably overreacted. He shot his wife in the eye, which didn't kill her, as he had intended, but no doubt made her think that conspiring with the Pope to poison her husband probably wouldn't have been a bad idea after all.

Col. Griffith spent two years in San Quentin where we can only hope he found other paranoid psychotics to spend quality time with. His legacy to the city involves more than just Griffith Park. He also willed enough money to the city to build a Greek Theater, an observatory, and a hall of science to be built on Mt. Hollywood. The Greek Theater was completed in September 1930. The observatory and hall of science were completed five years later.

But by that time, Col. Griffith J. Griffith lay a-mouldering in his grave. He had died of "liver failure" (Sure, that's what they *say!*) in 1919. Neither his wife nor the Pope attended his funeral.

# Mulholland Drive

On November 5, 1913, the hills north of San Fernando were crowded with 30,000 people. They were there to mark the moment in history when a desert would become a garden. Dug into the side of one of the mountains was a huge aqueduct, winding its way down the slope like a dry riverbed. It wasn't dry for long. Suddenly, with a roar—both from the water and the crowd—millions of gallons of mountain waters from the Owens Valley came coursing down the aqueduct. The job had taken five years and 5,000 workers and over $24 million. But from that day on, the San Fernando Valley and the city of Los Angeles had water.

The engineer in charge of this amazing feat was William Mulholland. He had been working on the aqueduct since 1907 when the Los Angeles government approved a $23 million bond to bring water south from the Sierra Nevada, 250 miles away. Mulholland was the superintendent of the Los Angeles water system which, in 1907, was a little like being Snowflake Manager of Greater Miami. However, after the water started to flow from the north, Los Angeles treated him like a hero.

The people in the Owens Valley weren't nearly so taken with him, however. Mulholland's siphoning off of their water supply

*William Mulholland*

ruined the entire area, turning the once green valley into a dust bowl. It took years for the California government to make reparations to the area, but by then most of the inhabitants had left.

Mulholland lived the high life for a decade or so. From 1924 to 1926 he oversaw the construction of the St. Francis Dam. This magnificent structure was another feather in Mulholland's cap until March 12, 1928, when the dam collapsed, killing some 380 people. Mulholland, who had never received an engineering degree, sank into a depression that would last until his dying day, in 1935.

A man as important as William Mulholland to the history of Los Angeles should certainly be honored by a monument of some kind, and so he is. Appropriately for a man who helped bring water to the area, Mulholland is memorialized by a fountain, located at the entrance to Griffith Park at Riverside and Memorial Drive.

He is also, of course, remembered by the spectacular roadway which bears his name. Mulholland Drive begins at the Cahuenga Pass in Hollywood and ends some fifty miles away, through the Santa Monica Mountains. Some of Los Angeles' most spectacular mansions line Mulholland Drive at its most populated spots, but there are densely rural sections, too.

Today, from any point atop the high, winding Mulholland Drive, you can get spectacular views of both Los Angeles and the San Fernando Valley; views that would be quite different—for better or worse—if not for the life and work of the man who gave the road its name.

# Verdugo Boulevard

Jose Maria Verdugo was a corporal in the Spanish army. He applied to Governor Pedro Fages for a land grant and, on October 20, 1784, received 86,000 acres. Although he had actually wanted a *lot* of property, Jose Maria was a philosophical man and took what he could get. He retired to his land in 1798 and became a cattleman. Sections of Burbank, Glendale, Highland Park, Eagle Rock, Verdugo Hills, and Sun City today occupy a part of Verdugo's land grant. Much of the property was eventually obtained by David Burbank, about whom you can read elsewhere in this chapter. Verdugo Boulevard runs west to east from Burbank to Glendale.

These days, if you ask the government to give you 86,000 acres of California real estate, chances are they will tell you no.

# Wilshire Boulevard

Henry Gaylord Wilshire was born with an oily spoon in his mouth. His father was a Cincinnati banker who had invested in oil, becoming so wealthy that his son nearly became a dismal failure. Gaylord flunked out of Harvard, then tried to manage a mill in Cincinnati. He did so badly at this job that he left town in shame and went where every failure and malcontent ends up— California.

Arriving in Southern California in 1886, Gaylord used his family money to start purchasing land at a terrifying rate (does buying up the entire shorefront of Long Beach seem excessive? Not to Gaylord!), and before you can say megalomania, he was running for Congress in 1890. He didn't make it, instead settling merely for untold wealth as an entrepreneur and rancher. In 1895 it occurred to Gaylord to develop a boulevard which would stretch from downtown Los Angeles all the way out to the beach at Santa Monica. He actually only developed the first four blocks of it, but it's the thought that counts, and today that long stretch is called Wilshire Boulevard.

# The City of Burbank

For most of my life, I assumed that the city of Burbank was named for horticulturalist Luther Burbank. After all, Luther *was* sort of the prototypical Californian. Working in Santa Rosa, he created whole slews of new vegetables and flowers and, like, communed with nature and stuff.

But in reality, although something certainly *should* be named for Luther, the city of Burbank was named for David Burbank. Why? Because he owned the land. David was a dentist, and apparently a darned good one, since he lived his life about chest deep in cash. If there was any frustration in his life, it was that he was only about fifty root canals away from owning the entire San Fernando Valley.

In 1867 Burbank bought the El Providencia Rancho —4,064 acres—from Alexander Bell and David Alexander, the first Anglos to receive title land in the San Fernando Valley. They had, in turn, purchased the land in 1843 for a whopping thirty-five cents an acre and doubled their money when they saw Deep Pockets Burbank coming.

Combining this property with another rancho he owned, San Rafael, David Burbank found himself with some 9,000 acres. This, of course, was too much property, even for a dentist. He raised sheep on the land for a few years, but then he began to aspire to something even bigger and grander than a sheep farm. In 1887 Burbank established the Providencia Land, Water and Development Company, a project that brought him a $250,000 return on his original $9,000 investment, not counting the sheep. He began subdividing his land, establishing a townsite which he modestly named for himself.

The Providencia company started the growth of the city of Burbank, and within two decades the place was blessed with a new hotel, a horse-drawn car line, a newspaper, and a bank. And, we can presume, a dentist's office.

# Wilcox Avenue

We can't look into the minds of others—particularly if those others have been dead for several decades—but it's a pretty safe bet that the avenue named for Horace Henderson Wilcox and his wife Daeida would not now make either one of them jump for joy; Wilcox Avenue in Hollywood is pleasant enough in some spots and an urban hell-hole in others. But either way you look at it, Mr. and Mrs. Wilcox envisioned something quite different for the area.

When they purchased a fig and apricot orchard, and the surrounding 160 acres, in 1887, they fostered dreams of building a new city. It would have a foundation of Christian faith and there would be no saloons or liquor stores. Any Protestant church which wished to set up shop within the city limits could have the land for free.

Oh, but what to call this Utopian community? Daeida had an idea.

Some time earlier, Mrs. Wilcox had been traveling east by train. She struck up a conversation with a woman from Chicago who told her all about her lovely estate, which she called Hollywood. Mrs. Wilcox thought that had a kind of ring to it. And so that's what she named her new city—Hollywood.

By 1899 Hollywood had about 500 residents. Within a decade the "movies"—which, at the time referred both to the films themselves and the people who made them— had come to town, and the Wilcox's Utopia didn't stand a chance.

Horace died in 1891. Daeida lived until 1914, long enough to see the first wave of the invasion of the movies.

Today, you will be shocked to learn, it is possible to find both saloons and liquor stores within the Hollywood city limits.

# Pico Boulevard

Governor Pio Pico

Pio Pico was the last Mexican governor of California (to date). He served two terms, in 1832 and 1845. Pio had the bad luck to be in office throughout the Mexican War of 1846-48, a result of which was that Mexico lost all of its California properties to the United States, which doesn't look that great on a governor's resume.

His brother Andres Pico actually seems to have been the most active and notable member of the family. Andres was a major landowner who leased the lands surrounding the former Mission de San Fernando in what is now called Mission Hills. There, for two decades, he raised longhorn cattle.

As more and more Americans drifted into California, Pio, in 1846, sold off all the missions to dictate, he said, "the measures [he] judged necessary for the defense of the Mexican nation." Pio granted the 117,000 acres of San Fernando Mission to a Spaniard, Eulogio de Celis, apparently in order to raise money to resist the American invasion. Andres bought half interest in the land in 1854 for $15,000. Later, he transferred his interest to Pio who sold it in 1869 to the two Isaacs: Lankershim and Van Nuys of the San Fernando Valley Homestead Association.

The "Andres Pico Adobe," built circa 1834, still stands about a quarter mile away from the Mission. Both buildings had lapsed into ruins over the years but were restored in the 1930s. Despite its name, Andres probably never lived in the house, although his son and daughter-in-law, Romulo and Catarina, did.

Pio lived on the grounds of the San Fernando Mission for many years. In 1845 he complained bitterly about the encroaching Americans who, he said, were "cultivating farms, establishing vineyards, sawing up lumber, building workshops...What are we then to do? Shall we remain supine, while those daring strangers are over-running our fertile plains, and gradually outnumbering and displacing us? Shall these incursions go unchecked until we shall become strangers in our own land?"

Apparently, the answer he came up with was "Yes." Pio Pico eventually sold all of his vast land holdings to American developers.

# Lankershim Boulevard and the City of Van Nuys

Isaac Newton Van Nuys and Isaac Lankershim

Two of the major American land developers to whom Pio Pico sold out were Isaac Lankershim and his son-in-law, Isaac Newton Van Nuys, two of the owners of the San Fernando Homestead Association. The two Isaacs were either incredibly industrious or ruthless and cold-blooded, depending on which side of the deal you were on. After purchasing the entire southern half of the San Fernando Valley from Pio Pico they controlled vast amounts of great farming land and potential residential areas.

At least they thought it was great farming land. Lankershim and Van Nuys tried raising sheep on several thousand of their newly acquired acres, but when a devastating drought resulted in the deaths of 40,000 sheep, the Isaacs began to rethink their plan. They had better luck raising wheat, although it took well over a decade for success to come.

In 1887 Lankershim bought 12,000 additional acres and formed the Lankershim Ranch Land and Water Co. He sold the subdivided land in forty-acre parcels, priced at $5 to $150 an acre.

Part of their holdings included a little community, just across the Cahuenga Pass from Hollywood, called Toluca. In 1896 Lankershim felt that he could come up with a better name for the town and, after considering the options, settled on Lankershim. The new name must have worked, for the town flourished. In fact, by 1920 things were growing so fast that residents had to put numbers on their houses. Only seven years later, in order to co-opt a little of the glamour from over the hill, the town's name was changed again, this time to North Hollywood. Now, the only landmark to Lankershim's land-shark legacy is Lankershim Boulevard, which cuts a diagonal swath through the Valley. In the seventies, even that was almost taken from him. A movement started to change the street's name to Universal Boulevard. It didn't work.

Isaac's son-in-law Isaac's name is still attached to the city of Van Nuys, founded on February 22, 1911. While it has its positive points, a drive through Van Nuys will make you wonder if it was really progress to build all this urban sprawl ("More Mini-Marts Than There Are In Heaven") over the harsh, beautiful landscape that first greeted the eyes—and excited the greed—of the two Isaacs: Lankershim and Van Nuys.

## A Few More Place Names

Alvarado Street for Juan B. Alvarado, once governor of California.

Sepulveda Boulevard for Francisco Sepulveda, acting mayor of Los Angeles in 1825.

Culver City for developer Harry Culver.

Sherman Oaks for developer General M.H. Sherman.

Tarzana for Tarzan, created by Edgar Rice Burroughs, whose estate was located on this property.

Downey for Governor John G. Downey, once owner of the land.

Bel-Air for developer Afonso Bell.

# L.A. Firsts

It's always risky to say that anything is the first anything.

I first learned this through my study of the movies. Reading some of the accepted histories of film, I was taught that *The Great Train Robbery* (1903) was the first story film. *Judith of Bethulia* (1909) was the first multi-reel feature. *Gertie the Dinosaur* (1914) was the first cartoon. *The Jazz Singer* (1927) was the first talkie. *Becky Sharp* (1935) was the first color film.

Of course, none of the above is true; so much for the accepted histories of film. Yet here I am, blithely starting up a chapter called "L.A. Firsts." All I can say is, these firsts *appear* to be genuine, and I've done my best to track them each down to the source. Still, you might want to take them with a grain of salt. And if you write in with angry challenges to my claims, I'll take your letters with a grain of salt, too.

# First Movie Studio

A tough one. Movies began drifting into California before the turn of the century, and the term "movie studio" can be defined in pretty broad terms. American Mutoscope and Biograph, a New York company, opened a Los Angeles branch in 1906. A year later, actor Francis Boggs brought a company from Chicago's Selig Company to Los Angeles and began making movies in a vacant lot at the Corner of Olive and Seventh. Selig built its first studio at 1845 Alessandro St. in 1909.

The first movie studio built in Hollywood seems to have been Nestor, the West Coast branch of the Centaur Company, located at 6101 Sunset Boulevard, on the site now occupied by CBS TV Channel 2. Why did Nestor come West to Hollywood? Film historian Kevin Brownlow, in his landmark book on silent cinema *The Parade's Gone By*, explains: "Centaur's chief director, Al Christie, had been making Westerns in the East, in Bayonne, New Jersey, and he had begun to tire of the inaccurate local backgrounds. He was anxious to try shooting in California but [Centaur co-owner] David Borsley felt that Florida would offer better climate and terrain. Christie tossed a coin, and California won."

# First Movie

*The Power of the Sultan* (1907) is generally accepted as the first dramatic film to be filmed entirely in California—to be specific, at 751 South Olive, at the corner of Olive and Seventh. It was made by Selig's Francis Boggs and starred Hobart Bosworth.

*Sultan's* ranking as Hollywood's first movie is, of course, disputed. Others believe the title should go to *The Heart of a Racing Tout* (1909), which is also credited to Boggs.

The first feature film to be produced entirely in Hollywood was probably Cecil B. De Mille's *The Squaw Man* (1914). Some of it was filmed in a barn at 1521 N. Vine at the corner of Vine and Selma [see "Movie Studios" chapter].

# First Movie Premiere

Sid Grauman had a knack for starting Hollywood traditions. In 1927 he would have movie stars leave their hand and footprints in the famous forecourt of his Chinese Theater. Four years earlier, he started another tradition that survives to this day: the movie premiere. Significantly, Douglas Fairbanks was involved in both occasions. Along with Norma Talmadge and his wife Mary Pickford, Fairbanks stepped into the wet cement at Grauman's Chinese; and his epic feature *Robin Hood* (1922) was chosen for the gala opening treatment at Grauman's Egyptian Theater. *Robin Hood*, directed by Hollywood veteran Allan Dwan, was one of the biggest, grandest epics of its time and is still terrifically entertaining today. The Egyptian Theater, on the other hand, isn't what it used to be. Boarded up and nearly forgotten, it retains only a hint of the fabulous glamour that was born at that glittering first movie premiere in 1923.

*Douglas Fairbanks in* Robin Hood—*first movie premiere.*

# First Home

"The Outpost," General Harrison Gray Otis' adobe house, has been called Hollywood's first home. Located at what is now 1903 Outpost Drive in the Hollywood Hills, the Outpost was the site, in 1847, of the signing of the peace treaty that ended the Mexican War. General Otis was the founder of the *Los Angeles Times*. He bought the property in the late 1800s and lived there until his death in 1917. The Outpost was torn down by developers in the mid-twenties.

Of course, the generations of Indians and Mexicans who lived in the area for centuries might find it slightly ironic to learn that the "first home" wasn't built until the nineteenth century.

The oldest standing home is the Avila Adobe, built in 1818, which now stands, virtually unchanged, on Olvera Street.

# First Movie Theater

On April 16, 1902, an item on the front page of the *Los Angeles Times* read:

ELECTRIC THEATER, 262 S. Main, opp. 3rd St.
New Place of Amusement

Up to date high class moving picture entertainment, especially for ladies and children. See the *Capture of the Biddle Bros.*, *New York, in a Blizzard*, and many other interesting and exciting scenes. An hour's amusement and genuine fun for

10 CENTS ADMISSION
Evenings: 7:30 to 10:30

The advertisement did the trick. Theater owner Thomas L. Tally immediately began offering afternoon matinees for the children, "five cents admission."

The Electric Theater was incredibly successful, but when Edwin S. Porter's pioneering Western *The Great Train Robbery* came along in 1903, Tally sold the theater and took the film on the road.

Most historians agree that the Electric Theater was Los Angeles' first movie theater. Some even insist it was the *country's* first.

# First Academy Awards Ceremony

On January 11, 1927 Metro-Goldwyn-Mayer's Louis B. Mayer invited thirty-six Hollywood hotshots to a formal banquet at the Ambassador Hotel (3400 Wilshire Boulevard). There he introduced his idea to form the "International Academy of Motion Picture Arts and Sciences." At its heart, Mayer's Academy was intended to be an organization which could mediate disputes with the motion picture labor unions which were rapidly gaining power. But the guests at this special dinner were swept up in some of its loftier ideals.

The Academy (which eventually dropped the "International" from its name) became a legal entity on May 4, 1927, and its first president, Douglas Fairbanks, sold some 300 memberships at $100 apiece.

Somewhere along the line it was decided that "awards of merit for distinctive achievement" were in order, and in no time Fairbanks had a committee making up rules for such an award. On the evening of May 16, 1929, a banquet was held in the Blossom Room of the Hollywood Roosevelt Hotel at 7000 Hollywood Boulevard, and there the first Academy Awards were given. Today, the

Academy Awards ceremonies are of interminable length, but that night, all the statuettes were handed out in about five minutes, flanked by a fancy dinner beforehand and an impromptu concert by Al Jolson afterwards.

# First Outdoor Shopping Mall

6671 Sunset Boulevard, Hollywood

On October 29, 1936 an unusual shopping area opened to the public. Crossroads of the World was designed by architect Robert V. Derrah for owner Ella Crawford. Because space was at a premium on busy Sunset Boulevard, Derrah designed a mall which would be closed to traffic and which would allow many more store fronts. An art deco neon sign marked the entrance. Atop the sign stood a sixty-foot tower on which an eight-foot globe revolved. On one side of the mall, the buildings were designed in Spanish fashion; on the other, the architecture was French and German. Farther up the street, the design becomes Moorish and Turkish. The entrance from Los Palmas is a crooked,

*Crossroads of the World in 1936*

narrow Cape Cod-like alleyway.

Crossroads of the World was declared a historical-cultural landmark in 1974. Today its stores have been converted into offices, but outwardly it looks much the same as it always has. It is one of Los Angeles' most whimsical and attractive landmarks.

## First Television Broadcast

5858 Sunset Boulevard

Announcer Dick Lane's voice and face were the first to be heard and seen on a television broadcast west of the Mississippi. The transmission originated from KTLA on January 22, 1947. For years, however, the center of television production remained in New York.

## First Gas Station

Los Angeles' car culture was already being established in 1912 when Earle Anthony opened his station at the corner of Grand Avenue and Washington Street. It was apparently not only L.A.'s first gas station, but the first in the United States. Little-known fact: by 1913, people were already complaining about the condition of the restrooms.

# Chapter V

# Unsolved Los Angeles Mysteries

There's a lot of talk throughout this book about the glamour of Los Angeles; but it has a very dark side as well. Maybe it's the extremes of which the city is capable that make it so endlessly fascinating. On the one hand it gave us the Keystone cops; on the other, the Manson Family. A beautiful actress like Thelma Todd can be living the high life at the Trocadero one night and dead of mysterious causes the next morning.

Sometimes it seems that people are even more interested in the ugly underbelly of Los Angeles than in its positive and beautiful aspects. Both of Kenneth Anger's *Hollywood Babylon* books, which revel in the seamy and tragic sides of the Tinseltown legend, have gained wide and continued popularity; a third volume is reportedly on the way. And thousands of people interested in personally inspecting the morbid sites of Hollywood murders and suicides and unsolved mysteries have taken a bus ride into mayhem with Grave Line Tours [call (213) 469-3127 or 469-4149 for information].

I suppose it's human nature to be intrigued by tales filled with horror, betrayal, or murder. And that intrigue is amplified when there's an element of mystery involved.

The stories that follow here have never been officially solved. From time to time books or articles are published, claiming to know the "true" story behind one or all of these crimes. But no one really knows for sure. And the farther we get away from them in time, the less likely it is that new evidence will appear to shed the light of truth on any of them.

Maybe that's for the best. Only someone with no imagination wants every question neatly answered. The rest of us prefer something a little more open-ended, sometimes. As we try to think the crime through, to examine clues and track down alibis, we close the distance between ourselves and the awful events. We cease acting only as spectators and become—if only in our imaginations—participants.

So try to solve some of these unsolved Los Angeles mysteries. Who knows? You just might crack one of the cases that have had the world baffled for decades....

# William Desmond Taylor

404 South Alvarado

William Desmond Taylor was one of Hollywood's top motion picture directors. Once an actor, he was still movie-star handsome at forty-five. Taylor had money, glamorous friends, fame, prestige. He also had enemies. And one of them crept into his Hollywood duplex late in the evening of February 1, 1922 and pumped two bullets into his back.

That Taylor's murder remains unsolved today is primarily due to the dizzying amount of covering-up that began the next morning with the discovery of his body. Before the police had even been called, representatives of Famous Players-Lasky (later known as Paramount

Pictures) went to Taylor's house and, so some say, began planting "evidence" all around, including pornographic pictures, a silk nightie (or, others say, silk panties), and love notes from famous actresses. One of these actresses, Sennett comedienne Mabel Normand, also got to the scene of the crime before police did, hunting frantically for something.

Normand was Taylor's close friend and claimed that she had written letters to him that might be misconstrued if made public. These letters were what she was searching for.

Another actress, 20-year-old Mary Miles Minter, was in love with Taylor and had been ardently pursuing him. Minter had a sweet, innocent screen persona, modeled on Mary Pickford, but, as so often happens, onscreen and offscreen personae didn't match perfectly. The newspapers reported that the nightie (or panties) found in Taylor's home bore the monogram "MMM."

Both Normand and Minter were considered suspects for a while, but police soon determined that neither of them would, or could, have murdered Taylor. Nevertheless, the publicity ruined both of their careers.

So who did kill William Desmond Taylor? The traditional answer in Hollywood folklore is Charlotte Selby, the mother of Mary Miles Minter. Selby was the mother of all stage mothers and it may be that she feared the scandal that would surely ensue if the world learned of her daughter's love affair with a man over twice her age. Another suggestion is that Selby was infuriated with Taylor for taking her daughter's virginity.

Others suggest that Taylor had ties with the underworld and was killed by the mob for informing to the police about drug traffic.

Still others suspect his manservant Henry Peavey who, it has been rumored, was Taylor's homosexual lover.

Taylor's home was demolished in 1966 to make room for a supermarket, which still stands on the spot.

At least two books have been written about the case (coming to entirely different conclusions) and hundreds of amateur sleuths have sifted through the evidence. But the answers remain elusive. The crime scene was so thoroughly tampered with by studio officials and others with something to hide that it was virtually worthless to police. And Taylor's private life was a maze of secrets and riddles. Any one of these dark places in his history might have contained things worth killing him for. All we know for sure is that someone killed William Desmond Taylor. And when he died, most of the innocence of Hollywood died with him.

## Paul Bern

9820 Easton Drive, Beverly Hills

Jean Harlow was one of the most beautiful and desirable stars of the thirties. Theoretically, she could have had her pick of any leading man. But when she married M-G-M producer Paul Bern on July 2, 1932, Hollywood raised an eyebrow in surprise. Although Bern was liked by many and respected by most, he was not what you'd call a handsome man. Short, with a receding hairline and no chin, Bern was also more than twice Harlow's age. Nevertheless, the couple seemed happy.

The happiness did not last. Just two months later, on the morning of September 5, Bern's nude body was found on the floor of their bedroom, his brains blown out by a single shot from a .38 which lay by his side. Harlow was away, visiting her mother.

Just as in the William Desmond Taylor case a decade earlier, the studio was contacted before the police were.

M-G-M executives Louis B. Mayer and Irving Thalberg were on the scene hours before official investigators arrived. Although it has been suggested that Harlow killed Bern and M-G-M quickly covered up all evidence of the crime, the truth seems to be that Mayer and Thalberg were simply making sure that their star would receive as little damage as possible to her career.

Bern's death was officially ruled a suicide, although many still consider it murder. The prime suspect is his former wife, Dorothy Millette.

In fact, to call Millette a "former" wife may not be quite accurate. Some historians argue that Bern was still married to her when he married Harlow. Millette had been quite ill and for many years was supported in an East Coast nursing home by Bern. One scenario has Millette arriving in Hollywood and confronting Bern, threatening to let the world know that he is a bigamist. They argue and she kills him. Another version repeats these events but ends with Bern killing himself in remorse. Yet another has Bern and Millette enjoying a very intimate reunion. Harlow catches them in the act and kills Bern.

Whatever really happened, only days later, Dorothy Millette leapt into a California river and drowned. Harlow had a stone erected at her grave and insisted that it read "Dorothy Millette Bern."

The house, which still stands, was purchased in 1968 by Jay Sebring, a Hollywood hairstylist. A year later, while visiting his friend Sharon Tate, Sebring was among those slaughtered by members of the Manson Family. As a result, the house is considered cursed by those who think in those terms. The current owners, however, seem to be doing fine.

# Thelma Todd

17531 Posetano Road

Thelma Todd had a vivacious screen presence and talent to burn. She was a brilliant comedienne who could—and did—hold her own with such formidable funny guys as Laurel and Hardy and the Marx Brothers. She could sing, dance, and act. Her vivaciousness carried over into her private life as well. Known to her friends as "Hot Toddy," she was friendly, likable, and exciting. Women adored her. Men lusted after her. And vice versa.

In 1934 she opened a restaurant with her friend, film director Roland West. Called Thelma Todd's Sidewalk Cafe, the place was located just across the Pacific Coast Highway from the beautiful Malibu beach [see Chapter XIV: "Restaurants and Night Spots" for more information about Thelma Todd's].

Thelma Todd seemed to be living the perfect Hollywood life. But it all ended sometime during the night of December 15-16, 1935. Entering the garage of Todd's home (owned by Roland West) at 17531 Posetano Road, the maid, Mae Whitehead, found Thelma's dead body in the front seat of her Lincoln convertible. Thelma sat upright and wore the blue silk evening gown she had worn the night before at a party at the Trocadero. Her fur coat rested on the seat beside her. She wore $20,000 worth of diamonds.

Authorities pronounced it accidental death due to carbon monoxide poisoning, apparently ignoring the fact that Todd's lower lip was discolored and that clots of dried blood were caked beneath her nostrils.

Suspicion rested on Roland West. Although his relationship with Todd had once been a love affair, it had since cooled down into a platonic friendship, based more on business than sex. But he was given the third-degree

*Thelma Todd*

by the police, who suspected that he had murdered her as part of a lover's quarrel.

The next suspect was Thelma's former husband, wealthy playboy Pasquale "Pat" De Cicco. He was known to have a violent streak, and their marriage had been stormy.

Later, it became known that Thelma had been approached by gangster "Lucky" Luciano, who wanted to establish a casino in the upper floor of the Sidewalk Cafe. Some theorize that she resisted his plan and was subsequently rubbed out, mob style.

Today, it seems most probable that West killed Thelma Todd, albeit accidentally. Historian Scott MacQueen suggests that West and Todd argued as she was about to drive out of the garage the night of December 15. To keep her home, he closed and locked the garage doors and stubborn Thelma sat there with the engine running, waiting for him to open them again. Neither of them, in the heat of the moment, considered the effect of the odorless carbon monoxide.

However, the death of the Hot Toddy is still unsolved. All the players in the drama are gone. All that's left are the house and garage where she died and the beautiful road house which she hoped would make her fortune. And, of course, the wonderful movies that she made.

## The Black Dahlia

3925 South Norton

One of the most baffling—and certainly the most gruesome—of unsolved Los Angeles mysteries began on the morning of January 15, 1947. A little girl, being walked to school by her mother, passed a weed-covered vacant lot on S. Norton Street, between Thirty-ninth and Coliseum. She noticed what appeared to be a broken department store mannequin. But her mother, taking a closer look, realized the horrible truth. It was the body of a woman, sawed neatly in half at the waist. The two body sections lay a couple of feet apart. Besides this rather expert surgery, the body had undergone numerous mutilations. The rope burns on her wrists and ankles indicated that the unfortunate victim had been tightly bound throughout her period of torture.

Oddly, the body had been entirely drained of blood, then meticulously bathed. It appeared that her hair had been dyed, shampooed, and set before her body was flung into the vacant lot.

Fingerprints revealed the victim's identity as Elizabeth Short, age twenty-two. Raised in Massachusetts, she had come out to Hollywood four years earlier, hoping for stardom. Instead, she became a prostitute.

*Elizabeth Short "The Black Dahlia"*

She was known around town as the Black Dahlia because of her habit of dressing entirely in black. She ran with a rough crowd, but, despite the biggest manhunt in Los Angeles history, the police were never able to connect any real suspects to the awful crime.

To date, over fifty people have confessed to killing the Black Dahlia. In the late 1980s, a woman came forward insisting that she had suppressed childhood memories of when her father tortured and killed Elizabeth Short. Official follow-ups to these claims have revealed nothing.

Today, nearly a half century after the ghastly crime, we seem to be no closer to solving it than ever.

## George Reeves

1579 Benedict Canyon, Beverly Hills

Late in the evening of June 15, 1959, a few friends stopped by George Reeves' modest home on Benedict Canyon Drive for a little nightcap. Lenore Lemmon, Reeves' fiancee, invited them in, and in no time the little party got pretty rowdy. Reeves, who had been trying to sleep, came storming downstairs, telling everyone to quiet down. He almost began exchanging blows with one of his inebriated guests. When Reeves was calmed down, he apologized and started back upstairs. Lenore said sarcastically, "Oh, he's going upstairs to kill himself." Within moments, a shot rang out. She said, calmly, "See? I told you. He's shot himself."

At least that's one version of the death of George Reeves, known around the world for his role on television's *Superman*. And it's the version that the authorities seem to have accepted. His death was ruled a suicide.

However, from the day of Reeves' death, many have believed that he was murdered. Why and by whom depend on whom you're talking to.

One suspect is Lenore Lemmon herself. All the guests there that night were quite drunk, and when police were questioning them, their stories changed by the minute. It has been suggested that Lenore slipped upstairs, killed Reeves, then came down and announced that he had killed himself. The guests were simply too drunk to dispute her.

*George "Superman" Reeves*

Another suspect is M-G-M executive Eddie Mannix. Reeves had been carrying on a long-time love affair with Mannix's wife, Toni, which ended only with Reeves' engagement to Lenore Lemmon. Oddly, a couple of months before his death, Reeves went to the Los Angeles District Attorney to claim that he had been receiving harassing phone calls and that he believed Toni Mannix was the culprit. No charges were filed and no proof was ever discovered to establish that the calls were made. But things get stranger, still. When Reeves' will was examined after his death, it was discovered that he had left everything to—Toni Mannix.

The truth seems to be that Eddie Mannix knew of and perhaps silently endorsed his wife's affair with Reeves.

He had no real motive for murder, unless he was angry at Reeves for breaking his wife's heart.

Which leads to the inevitable claim that Toni herself was the murderer. This doesn't hold much water either.

Reeves' mother claimed loudly and repeatedly that her son had been murdered. It was rumored that she kept his body on ice for several months, pending a reopening of the investigation.

Although the trail gets colder and colder as time passes, the most likely explanation for George Reeves' death is the simplest one: he committed suicide. His friends knew how depressed he was about the course of his career. Producers could see him only as Superman, and the only roles he could find were in low-budget pictures. It was said that he received word on the day of his death that a new season of *Superman* was about to go into production. Could this news have depressed him to such an extent that he actually killed himself? At least some of his friends think so. Others keep insisting that he was murdered and that the murder was covered up. While this isn't very likely, it's a theory that refuses to go away. Ironically, the mysterious circumstances of his death have kept George Reeves' name alive for decades—well, that and the endless reruns of *Superman*, the show he hated so much.

# Chapter VI

# The L.A. Tragedy Tour

Want to conduct your own Morbid Tour? Here's a list of some of the more notable locations that have seen grisly moments of one kind or another:

### 905 Loma Vista Drive, Beverly Hills

The Greystone Mansion. Later the home of the American Film Institute, in 1929 it was the site of a murder-suicide involving millionaire E.L. Doheny Jr. and his male secretary.

### 512 North Palm Drive

Jean Harlow died of uremic poisoning in 1937 at this address.

### 810 Linden Drive, Beverly Hills

Gangster Benjamin Siegel disliked being called "Bugsy." He was killed in this house by a series of shotgun blasts in 1947.

## 1465 Capri Drive, Beverly Hills

The house in which actress Carole Landis killed herself in 1948.

## 730 North Bedford, Beverly Hills

In 1958, Lana Turner's lover Johnny Stompanato was stabbed to death here by Turner's daughter, Cheryl Crane. After a sensational trial, the killing was ruled justifiable homicide.

## 8825 Hollywood Boulevard

The site of Lenny Bruce's last overdose in 1966.

## 5699 Valley Oak Drive, Studio City

The house in which Ramon Navarro, star of *Ben-Hur* (1925), was beaten to death by two drifters in 1968.

## 10050 Cielo Drive, Beverly Hills

(Note, in order to maintain privacy, the house number was subsequently changed to 10048 Cielo Drive).

Where Sharon Tate, Jay Sebring, and three others were slaughtered by members of the Manson Family in 1969.

## 3301 Waverly Drive, Glendale

The home of Leno and Rosemary LaBianca, the last two victims of the Manson Family in 1969.

## 8787 Shoreham Drive, West Hollywood

Art Linkletter's daughter Diane, high on LSD, jumped from the sixth floor of this building in 1969.

## 7047 Franklin Avenue, Hollywood

The Landmark Hotel is where Janis Joplin overdosed on heroin in 1970.

## 8563 Holloway Drive, West Hollywood

Actor Sal Mineo was stabbed to death in his carport here in 1976.

## 1221 North Kings Road, West Hollywood

Actor/singer Jack Cassidy, former husband of Shirley Jones, burned to death in his penthouse apartment at this address in 1976.

## 86575 Comstock Avenue, Westwood

Here's where comedian Freddie Prinze fatally shot himself in 1977.

## 9402 Beverly Crest Drive

The house in which Rock Hudson died in 1985.

## 722 North Elm, Beverly Hills

The site of one of the most sensational murders of the nineties—so far. Here is where Jose and Kitty Menendez were killed by multiple shotgun blasts in 1990. Their sons, Lyle and Eric, were arrested for the crimes.

## 875 North Bundy, Brentwood

In front of this condominium, Nicole Brown Simpson and her friend Ron Goldman were savagely murdered on June 12, 1994. It was the site of a media circus for months after the event. Nicole's former husband, O.J. Simpson, was arrested and tried for the crimes.

## 360 North Rockingham, Brentwood

O.J. Simpson's home in Brentwood became famous the world over during the long, tense day that he and friend Al Cowlings drove up the 405 Freeway toward it, followed by police cars, helicopters, media and—most surreally—crowds of well-wishers parked on every under-pass along the way. Simpson's white Ford Bronco was parked in front of this house for hours while police negotiated with him to surrender. He eventually did so, peacefully.

# Chapter VII

# The Movie Palaces

In director William A. Wellman's definitive Hollywood romance/tragedy *A Star Is Born* (1937), would-be actress Esther Blodgett (Janet Gaynor) arrives in Hollywood with dreams of glory. Her first stop is at that gaudy, tacky, wonderful monument to movie glamour, Grauman's Chinese Theater. She looks in awe at the handprints and footprints and autographs of the stars, preserved in the large squares of cement that make up the floor of the Chinese Theater's forecourt—"The Floor of Fame." When she sees the footprints of her favorite star, Norman Maine (Fredric March)—the man she will eventually marry—she can't resist stepping into them; Esther's in a total state of rapture.

Not many tourists, even sixty years later, can resist making that same pilgrimage and finding out just how their hands and feet compare to those of their cinematic idols. (Mine, if you must know, are larger than Harold Lloyd's but smaller than John Wayne's.) The Chinese Theater (now Mann's, not Grauman's) is a direct link to the Tinseltown past. You won't find a great deal in this city that even survives from the twenties and thirties, but the Chinese Theater looks a great deal like it has always looked.

Times have changed. Movie theaters are far more likely to be crammed by the dozen into the far end of a shopping mall than to be placed inside ornate temples of entertainment. But there are still a few other great old movie palaces around town. Some are still up and running, others are dark and boarded up, and still others—a precious few—have been restored to their former glory. So often in Hollywood, if you want to connect with the past, you have to use your imagination. But when you're watching a movie in the Chinese Theater or any of the other great old palaces, you're in exactly the right place to experience the Hollywood you've always dreamed of.

## Mann's Chinese Theater and the Legacy of Sid Grauman

6925 Hollywood Boulevard

Showman Sid Grauman (1879-1950) believed that the places where motion pictures were shown should be as eye-popping as the movies themselves. His fabulous Million Dollar Theater (which still stands at 307 South Broadway in downtown Los Angeles) was built in 1917, opening with a William S. Hart Western, *The Silent Man*. Its gargoyle-rich design is still impressive and fascinating, and the interior of the theater is today virtually unchanged. In 1922 Grauman opened his Egyptian Theater at 6708 Hollywood Boulevard with Douglas Fairbanks' latest epic *Robin Hood* (this was Hollywood's first movie premiere). Resembling a set out of a particularly weird Cecil B. De Mille epic, the Egyptian is closed today and looking pretty seedy.

Sid Grauman wanted his Chinese Theater to be the greatest of them all. Designed by architects Meyer and Holler, the Chinese is a magnificent melange of pagodas, spires, ornate carvings, and other faux Oriental design elements. When it opened in 1927, with De Mille's *King of Kings*, the Chinese was considered one of the most interesting and opulent of Hollywood's movie palaces. But it took that extra little dab of showmanship—"The Floor of Fame"—to turn the Chinese from simply one of

*Grauman's Chinese Theater, 1930*

the pack to one of the most recognized buildings in the world.

Just how the tradition got started of placing hand-prints and footprints in wet cement is a little hard to nail down. Some say a movie star (Norma Talmadge in most versions of the story) slipped while the theater was under construction and stepped in wet cement, and Sid Grauman liked what he saw. Others say that one of the masonry workers put his hand in cement as a signature. Grauman asked him what was going on, and the worker said that this is the way his ancestors in France "signed" the great cathedrals which they built.

Whatever the true story, on May 17, 1927, Grauman asked Norma Talmadge (she got there one way or the other!), Mary Pickford, and Douglas Fairbanks to place their hands and feet in cement. The stars showed up, but the press didn't. So everybody came back the next day and did it again.

In the ensuing seven decades nearly 200 celebrities have been offered this unique brand of immortality. Harold Lloyd placed the imprint of his famous glasses in his cement square; Jimmy Durante left an impression of his nose; Roy Rogers *and* Trigger signed in. So did *Star Wars'* robots R2D2 and C-3PO.

And when Janet Gaynor stepped in the footprints of the fictional Norman Maine in 1937, she must have experienced *deja vu*; the actress had left her own hand- and footprints there on May 29, 1929.

Because it seems that movie theaters with only one screen can no longer exist, a second screen was added to the Chinese a few years ago. But don't worry, the original theater was not altered; the other screen was simply added onto the east side of the building.

*Million Dollar Theater, ca. 1925*

# The Pantages—Old and Older

6233 Hollywood Boulevard, Hollywood
607 S. Hill, Los Angeles

This magnificent Art Deco structure was built in 1930 by architect Marcus Priteca, one of more than 500 theaters he designed. The first film that played there was a Marion Davies vehicle, *Floradora*. Although no longer a movie theater, much of the Pantages' original decor still exists, a poignant reminder of its former splendor. The Pantages gained national fame as the headquarters for the Academy Awards ceremonies from 1949 to 1959.

There was an earlier version of the Pantages, located at 607 S. Hill in Los Angeles. Now known as the Jewelry Mart, the old Pantages was as suffused with bad luck as its newer cousin would be with glamour. In 1923 "Choy Ling Foo Troupe," a Chinese vaudeville act, was appearing at the Pantages. The five members, who were cousins, apparently got along with the audience a lot better than they got along with each other. One night, as the audience sat waiting for the performance to begin, the troupe had a difference of opinion in the dressing room. The fire-eater pulled a pistol and killed the troupe's contortionist. He then placed the pistol to his own head and fired.

Six years later, in 1929, Alexander Pantages, owner of the theater, was accused of raping a seventeen-year-old girl in a second-story office. It is now generally believed that the accusation was a false one, but he was found guilty after a sensational trial. Pantages served two years in prison before the verdict was overturned in 1931.

Both of the Pantages theaters still exist in some semblance of their original beauty. Together, they represent both the bright and dark sides of Hollywood legend.

The Movie Palaces

# The Theater District

Broadway, between Third and Ninth streets

This area, now a little frayed around the edges, contains a remarkable collection of movie palaces. Many of them are still in operation, showing Spanish-language or subtitled films. Some of them occasionally show a special classic film, sometimes a silent movie with live musical accompaniment. Every one of them is worth a visit.

# The Orpheum

842 S. Broadway, Los Angeles

One Hollywood tour guide calls The Orpheum the "best preserved theater in Los Angeles" and the opinion is difficult to dispute. It still looks much as it did when it opened in 1925. The Orpheum was designed by G. Albert Landsburgh, a prolific architect whose surviving Los Angeles theaters also include *The Palace* (South Broadway, built in 1911). MTV fans will remember The Palace from the opening scenes of Michael Jackson's *Thriller* video.

# The Los Angeles

615 S. Broadway, Los Angeles

This rococo masterpiece opened its doors in 1931. Designed by S. Charles Lee, The Los Angeles' first movie was *City Lights*, starring and directed by Charlie Chaplin. The Los Angeles was, and is, a spectacular building. It boasted an art gallery, a nursery, restaurant, mahogany-paneled ballroom, fountain, and such modern features as remote control switchboards and aisles lit by neon.

*Los Angeles Theater, 1931*

## Other Theater District Treasures

The theaters discussed above are some of the most striking and important of the downtown movie palaces, but they are far from the only ones in the Theater District. Some of the other beautiful theaters include: The Roxie, 518 S. Broadway; The Globe, 744 S. Broadway; The Tower, 802 S. Broadway; The Mayan, 1044 S. Hill; and The Arcade, 534 S. Broadway.

The Los Angeles Conservancy, (213) 623-2489, offers regular walking tours of the area, an exercise that is highly recommended for anyone who wants a taste of a past era of splendor. The Conservancy is dedicated to preserving these theaters and, we can only hope, to their eventual restoration.

# Chapter VIII

# L.A. Landmarks: Past and Present

## Beverly Hills Hotel

9641 Sunset Boulevard

Old-timers call it "The Pink Palace." The Eagles, in their hit song, called it "The Hotel California." Howard Hughes called it a home away from home. So did Marilyn Monroe. Clark Gable and Carole Lombard made Bungalow #4 their illicit love nest in the thirties before his divorce was final. But whatever you call it, the Beverly Hills Hotel is one of the most conspicuous and longest-lived of elegant Hollywood landmarks. Built in 1912, the hotel was, from the beginning, the perfect stopping place for stars who were waiting for homes to be completed in the area. Some actors would never admit that they had Gone Hollywood and stayed in the hotel for months at a time, waiting until they could finish with the high-paying movies and get back to their real calling: the New York Stage.

The hotel's Polo Lounge has always been a prime place for doing business, signing deals, making connections. Hollywood hopefuls walk very slowly through the lounge, hoping to catch the eye of some big director or influential agent. Failing that, they'll fall back on the old standby of having themselves paged, loudly and repeatedly, until everyone in the room has heard their name.

The rooms in the Hollywood Hotel proper are expensive by any rational standards, but they seem quite reasonable when compared to the shady, private little bungalows that surround the place; those rent for $1,000 to $3,000 a night. Howard Hughes used to rent one of these by the year.

In recent years the Pink Palace had begun to look a little faded around the edges. The Sultan of Brunei bought it in 1987 and decided to give the old girl a facelift. At this writing, the Beverly Hills Hotel is closed for a two-year remodeling job that is said to be budgeted at more than $100 million. It's set to open again in 1995, restored to its former opulence, pinker than ever.

*The Beverly Hills Hotel*

# Hollywood High School

1521 North Highland

When the cornerstone of Hollywood High was laid on November 23, 1904, the corner of Sunset and Highland was a lovely rural area. The first classes were overwhelmingly composed of Caucasian students. They tethered their horses on one side of the campus, and lemon groves covered another side.

Today, the school's population speak nearly sixty languages. No longer possessing a lovely, pastoral campus, Hollywood High stands amid urban squalor. But it can look back on an eventful nine decades of existence. In 1917, just before America entered the First World War, the athletic fields of Hollywood High were used for training soldiers. For years it served a variety of civic functions.

But Hollywood High is best known for its notable alumni, who range from Nobel prize-winning chemist William Shockley, *Los Angeles Times* publisher Norman Chandler, and Episcopal Bishop James J. Pike to such stellar names in entertainment as Carol Burnett, Jason Robards, Rick and David Nelson, and James Garner. It was while Lana Turner was a Hollywood High student that she was discovered, sipping a soda at the Top Hat Malt Shop—*not*, as Hollywood legend has it, at Schwab's Drug Store (which stood at 8024 Sunset Boulevard until 1985)—by the *Hollywood Reporter*'s Jimmy Wilkerson. When Wilkerson asked the sixteen-year-old Turner if she wanted to be in the movies she replied, "I don't know. I'll have to ask my mother."

# Farmer's Market

300 North Fairfax

In 1934, in the midst of the Great Depression, Roger Dahlhjelm had a great idea. Noting the high price of fresh produce, fruits, and vegetables, Dahlhjelm gathered together a group of farmers and suggested that they find an empty piece of land and establish an informal market where they could sell their goods directly to the public without middlemen. Oilman Earl Gilmore offered part of his land at Third and Fairfax, and by July 1934, the Farmer's Market was up and running.

Today, the Farmer's Market remains one of the "musts" of any tour of Los Angeles. There are now permanent buildings, including book, clothing, jewelry, and toy stores, and one long building is taken up with an indoor flea market. But the heart of the place is still the canvas-roofed stands which sell everything from fresh fruit to sausages to suitcases. The many restaurants that dot the place offer some great food at very reasonable prices; having a hearty, open-air breakfast at one of the counters is a quintessential Hollywood experience.

Also on the property stands Earl Gilmore's adobe home, one of Los Angeles' oldest houses. The house was built in 1852 and Gilmore was born there in 1887. He died in 1964, in the same bed in which he was born. When his widow died in the seventies, the adobe house became the information center for the Farmer's Market; for all these reasons, it's a fascinating place to visit.

# Capitol Records Tower

1750 North Vine

Almost any good view of the Hollywood skyline (such as it is) is marked by this unique, thirteen-story circular building. Completed in 1956, the Capitol Records Tower was built to look like a stack of records. It was conceived by singer Nat King Cole and songwriter Johnny Mercer, but architect Welton Becket actually designed and built it. On the first floor, there is a mural of some of Capitol's greatest recording artists, including Frank Sinatra, the first singer to record in the Tower's studios.

# Ambassador Hotel/Cocoanut Grove

3400 Wilshire Boulevard

The impressive Ambassador Hotel opened on January 1, 1921. It was set upon a hill so that—in those less crowded times—guests could have an unobstructed view in every direction. The rich and famous soon filled many of the Ambassador's 400 rooms, and the popularity of the Zinnia Grill, the hotel casino, and a small dance club called the Black Patent Leather Room led the management to consider putting in a first-class nightspot.

The hotel's grand ballroom was chosen as the most logical site, and on April 21, 1921, Hollywood's newest hot spot opened: the Cocoanut Grove. The Grove was decorated with fake palm trees which had been purchased from the production of Rudolf Valentino's film *The Sheik*. In each of these trees sat a stuffed monkey.

In no time, the Cocoanut Grove was the place to be; columnists called it "The Playground of the Stars." Charles Chaplin sometimes improvised a little entertainment. Joan Crawford and Carole Lombard danced the Charleston. The Grove's reign continued through the thirties when regulars included Fred Astaire, Al Jolson, Jack Benny, Dick Powell, George Raft, Alice Fay, Ginger Rogers, Jerome Kern, and many other top-rank celebrities.

After the Second World War, the Cocoanut Grove lost some of its luster as a new generation of stars found new hot nightclubs; but the Grove remained active—a lush reminder of better times—into the eighties.

The Ambassador, of course, gained an entirely different kind of reputation in 1968, when Senator Robert Kennedy was assassinated there after having given a presidential campaign speech. Threatened with demolition in 1988, the Ambassador was bought by Donald Trump and, as of this writing, is undergoing renovation. It may be that soon, both this remarkable hotel and the glamorous, nostalgic nightclub in its grand ballroom will once again sparkle as they did in those Charleston-filled nights so many years ago.

# The Hollywood Sign

Atop Mount Lee, Hollywood Hills

This huge white sign, which looks down on Hollywood from the hills to the north, is, without serious competition, the single most recognizable landmark in the city. Its crooked lettering may as well be the registered trademark logo of Hollywood.

That the Hollywood sign began life as an advertising billboard for a planned community called "Hollywoodland" is itself pretty appropriate. It's an advertising billboard, still; only now the sign is selling not property but a state of mind. And millions of people around the world, past and present, have bought what the sign has to sell.

Hollywoodland began life in 1923 when developers sold the first 120 lots in the Hollywood Hills. The huge sign was built later in the same year. Each of the thirteen letters was fifty feet high, thirty feet wide, and constructed of sheet metal, pipe, wire, and telephone poles. It was illuminated with 5,000 forty-watt bulbs and cost $21,000 to build.

Originally, the sign lit up in sequence: first HOLLY; then WOOD; then LAND; and finally the whole thing, all at once. It made quite an impressive sight up in those nearly empty hills and helped establish Hollywoodland as a desirable place to own a home.

The sign was not built to last. A good gust of wind could knock down a letter or two—and frequently did.

In 1932 the sign truly entered Hollywood folklore when actress Peg Entwhistle, despondent over how poorly she thought her career was going, climbed to the top of one of the letters and jumped to her death. News reports state that she leapt from the H, but the correct letter has been transformed over the years to the more eerie final D—the thirteenth letter.

The last four letters were torn down in the forties, and the City of Los Angeles took over the ownership of the sign. Its condition deteriorated alarmingly over the years until 1978, when the sign was restored with donated funds supplied by, among others, Hugh Hefner, Alice Cooper, and Gene Autry.

Today the Hollywood sign is 50 feet high, 450 feet long, and weighs 480,000 pounds.

# The Hollywood Bowl

2301 Highland

The land where the Hollywood Bowl now sits was known in 1918 as Daisy Dell. This pleasant-sounding place attracted the eye of Christine Witherill Stevenson, an heiress to the Pittsburgh Paint fortune, who made it her personal duty to bring culture to Los Angeles. Chiefly, Ms. Stevenson wanted to accomplish this through religious plays, but she also thought concerts of uplifting music might do the trick as well. With the aid of a couple of friends, she purchased Daisy Dell for $49,000 in September 1919.

The first concert held at the site was performed by a contralto, accompanied by piano. Both were placed on a hastily constructed wooden platform; their purpose was to test the acoustics of the meadow. The acoustics, everyone agreed, were fine.

Concerts were performed as early as 1920, before the distinctive domed amphitheater was built. One of its first performers was actor Lionel Barrymore who, with the Hollywood Community Chorus, gave the audience "The Landing of the Pilgrims."

The first actual concert season began in August 1921, and the Bowl's first shell was constructed a year later. A series of replacement shells have gone up over the years, including a couple in the mid-twenties designed by Frank Lloyd Wright. By the end of 1929, the shell which is still in use was built at a cost of $35,000.

Ms. Stevenson purchased twenty-nine acres across the Cahuenga Pass from the Hollywood Bowl to put on her religious plays. Her theater continued to function there until the 1960s when it became the John Anson Ford County Cultural Arts Theater, now the home of the Los Angeles Shakespeare Festival.

When Ms. Stevenson died in 1922, a lighted cross was erected in her honor atop a hill overlooking her theater. It was damaged by fire in 1965 and replaced with a new model that's still there today.

*The Hollywood Bowl*

## The Chateau Marmont

8221 Sunset Boulevard

The charming little bungalows of the Chateau Marmont Hotel began life as apartments in 1927. The casual mood of privacy has always made the Marmont a favorite retreat for stars—from Garbo to Monroe to

De Niro—who want to avoid the limelight. It was also traditionally a place for hanky panky. Columbia studio head Harry Cohn used to tell his stars, "If you must get into trouble, do it at the Marmont."

Of course, some people found a little too much trouble in this quaint little hideaway. The most notable of Marmont tragedies was the death of *Saturday Night Live*'s John Belushi on March 5, 1982. Belushi died of an overdose of cocaine and heroin in Bungalow #2.

But the Chateau Marmont has happier memories, too. Paul Newman and Joanne Woodward reportedly began their romance there; so did Sam Shepard and Jessica Lange. And it continues to be favored by up-and-comers with modest tastes and plenty of cash—charming it is; cheap it ain't.

# The Garden of Allah

8152 Sunset Boulevard

Just across Sunset Boulevard from the Chateau Marmont once stood one of the most beautiful and interesting of Hollywood hotels. The Garden of Allah was once the home of the exotic Russian silent film actress Alla Nazimova. When she was on top (making a reported

THE GARDEN OF ALLAH
HOTEL AND VILLAS
8152 SUNSET BOULEVARD  •  • HOLLYWOOD, CALIF.

$13,000 a week in the teens) Nazimova's home was a social center. But her fortunes took a turn for the worse in the early twenties, and she was forced to sell her beloved home. The new owners were kind enough to allow Nazimova to continue living in an apartment in the house. Then they built twenty-five guest cottages and began to operate the place as a hotel. They named it the Garden of Allah, after Nazimova, but, of course, misspelled her first name.

From the beginning, the Garden of Allah attracted Hollywood's intelligentsia, most of whom were New Yorkers, temporarily and rather unwillingly imprisoned by the movies. Writers and wits like Robert Benchley, F. Scott Fitzgerald, and Dorothy Parker lived here; in fact, the Garden of Allah has often been called a West Coast version of the famous Algonquin Round Table.

Movie stars like Orson Welles and Errol Flynn also stayed in the Garden of Allah's bungalows.

The hotel was torn down in 1959. The site is today occupied by a mini-mall. In the lobby of the Great Western Bank on the property is a scale model of the grand home/hotel which once stood there.

# Pickfair

1143 Summit Drive

In 1920 Douglas Fairbanks and Mary Pickford were two of the most famous movie stars in the world. When they married, they became known as the King and Queen of Hollywood. Doug bought a massive hunting lodge, with fifteen acres, on Summit Drive in Beverly Hills, remodeled it, and gave it to Mary as a wedding present. In no time flat the place was known as Pickfair.

The King and Queen of Hollywood attracted genuine royalty to their twenty-two-room mansion: King Umberto of Italy, England's Lord and Lady Mountbatten, and the King and Queen of Siam stayed there. With the exception of their close friend Charlie Chaplin and performers like Greta Garbo and Rudolph Valentino, Pickfair did not host that many movie people. More to Doug and Mary's taste were guests such as George Bernard Shaw, Albert Einstein, and the President of the United States, Calvin Coolidge.

Pickfair boasted a 100-foot-long swimming pool, complete with a sandy beach and canoe. Inside the house were drawings by Rodin, jade carvings, and a set of china once given by Napoleon to Josephine.

Doug and Mary divorced in 1935, and two years later she married Charles "Buddy" Rogers. After her death in 1979, Buddy moved to the edge of the property in a spacious home modestly called "the Lodge."

Pickfair was then sold to Jerry Buss, the owner of the Los Angeles Lakers, and, in 1988, went to Meshulam Riklis, the husband of singer Pia Zadora for $6.6 million. Riklis has remodeled Pickfair until it is barely recognizable as the beautiful home that once played host to kings and queens, both official and honorary. Beyond its altered appearance, it isn't a recommended tourist spot, simply because it's virtually impossible to see the house over the massive wall that surrounds the property.

But if you catch it at just the right time of day, and you listen closely, maybe you can hear the ghostly voices of those who had happy times here, when Pickfair was the center of the show business universe.

# Bradbury Building

304 South Broadway

From the outside, the Bradbury Building doesn't look like much, but inside it's one of the most remarkable and unusual buildings in the city. George H. Wyman designed the Bradbury in 1893, and its intricate patterns of steel, wrought-iron, marble, and dark wood are both evocative of the past and, somehow, timeless. The vaulted roof with an enormous skylight towers over the hydraulic, open-air elevators. If you're a moviegoer, you'll probably remember the Bradbury from films like *Blade Runner*, but even if you don't bring with you any familiarity with the building, you'll be amazed at its complex beauty.

The Bradbury Building was restored in the eighties and there is now a charge to go in, look around, and ride the elevators. It's only a couple of dollars and well worth it. The Bradbury Building is a true Los Angeles marvel.

## Olvera Street

400-500 South Main

If there is such a thing as a "historic heart" of a city, then that is what Olvera Street is to Los Angeles. Closed to automobile traffic since 1930, Olvera Street is a Mexican marketplace, offering all manner of shops, sidewalk vendors, restaurants, and historic exhibits in a single city block. The Avila Adobe, Los Angeles' oldest existing house, built in 1818, is on Olvera Street. So is the beautiful Sepulveda House, constructed in 1887.

At the south end of Olvera Street stands La Iglesia, the city's oldest public building. Every Easter, a charming ceremony takes place at the Plaza Church, which was also built in 1818. The Blessing of the Animals invites children from all over the area to bring in their pets to be blessed by the priests. The wall leading up the hill from Alameda to Olvera is decorated with a mural depicting this custom.

Dancers, singers, and *mariachis* entertain on Olvera Street, and some of the buildings sometimes offer historical exhibits of photographs and artifacts from the history of the area. There are several good restaurants, too. One of them offers the weirdest dessert your humble author ever heard of: a scoop of ice cream topped with two Twinkies, all of which is covered with chocolate sauce. Of course, in the interest of cultural research, he purchased and ate it and only sort of regretted it later.

There are rumors that Olvera Street is about to receive restaurants from major chains such as Red Lobster or Sizzler in order to give the marketplace "a broader appeal." If you visit this evocative area, however, you'll know that it has all the appeal it needs. Olvera Street is a warm, lively, and interesting place. Besides, anyone who can offer Twinkies and ice cream soaked in chocolate syrup doesn't need culinary help from anybody.

# Union Station

800 North Alameda

When you've completed your tour of Olvera Street, step across Alameda to visit one of Los Angeles' most beautiful landmarks: Union Station. Just to step into this magnificent Spanish Revival masterpiece is to be transported to an era when train travel was not only enjoyable, but stylish and adventurous. The ceilings are fifty-two feet high, which gives the busy station an unlikely sense of quiet and serenity. The meticulously restored tile floors and mahogany-and-leather seats are always immaculate. It's always more fun to walk around Union Station when you don't actually have to catch a train. After this build-up of style (you keep expecting to see Cary Grant stroll through), boarding a dreary old Amtrak car is quite a let-down; what's really called for is a thirties-era Pullman car.

Union Station, designed by John and Donald Parinson, opened for business on May 7, 1939. For years it was the point of arrival for the famous Twentieth Century Limited, the cross-country train that always (if you believed the fan magazines) seemed to bring new stars to Hollywood from New York or Chicago.

Now owned by Santa Fe Pacific Realty, Union Station is constantly threatened with being turned into a shopping mall or hotel. But for now it is what it has always been and what it always should be: a magnificent cathedral of travel, a pristine window into the most sophisticated and charming moments of this city's not-always-charming past.

## More Landmarks

*The Witch's House*   516 Walden Drive, Beverly Hills. A weird fairy tale kind of cottage, built in the twenties as the administration building for the Willat Studios in Culver City and moved to this spot in 1930.

*The Silent Movie*   611 N. Fairfax Avenue. The only theater in the country devoted entirely to silent films. Charlie Chaplin used to come here in the forties to watch his old films. More recently, Johnny Depp frequented the place, studying Buster Keaton for his role in *Benny and Joon*.

*The Cinerama Dome*   6360 Sunset Boulevard. Built in 1963 to exhibit the ultra-widescreen Cinerama format, the Dome was too late for the short-lived phenomenon. The distinctive round building is still one of the most interesting movie theaters in town and a great place to see movies the way they should be seen—BIG.

*Ozzie and Harriet's House*   1822 Camino Palermo, Beverly Hills.

*The Magic Castle*   7001 Franklin, Hollywood. This ornate mansion, built in 1909, is now a members-only magicians' club. Non-magicians can only get in with an invitation from a member. The attractions range from close magic performed at your table to the "Houdini Seance," which recreates a classic seance with (literally) all the bells and whistles.

*Playboy Mansion*   10236 Charing Cross Road, Beverly Hills. As with the Magic Castle, you can only get in if you're invited. Most people who go there seem to like it for some reason. Built in 1927, it was purchased by Hugh Hefner in 1971. And if the walls could talk....

*The Watts Towers*   1765 East 107th Street, Watts. Although the Watts section is, unfortunately, best known for the disastrous riots of 1966, the neighborhood is also home to one of the most remarkable sculptures in Los Angeles. Created by Simon Rodia from 1921 to 1954, the

Watts Towers are 100 feet tall and constructed of metal, shells, tiles, glass, and cement. At the foot of the towers is the Watts Towers Arts Center which features exhibitions. Call (213) 847-4646.

*Westwood Village*   This is as close as you can come to a walking neighborhood in Los Angeles; upscale, but with brains. Built in the twenties, most of the buildings are designed in Spanish Colonial style. There are cafes, many bookstores, and restaurants of every description, as well as several wonderful movie theaters, particularly The Village and The Bruin, both on Broxton Avenue. Westwood Village is within an easy stroll of UCLA.

# Chapter IX

# Who Lives Here?
# L.A.'s Ethnic Makeup

Los Angeles is one of the great multiethnic cities of the world. Just name any race, religion, or national origin and you can not only find representatives living within the city, you can probably find a *lot* of them.

Caucasians still make up the majority in Los Angeles, but just barely. According to the 1990 Census, 49.7 percent of the population is Caucasian and 32.9 percent Hispanic. Asians make up the next highest ethnic population with 8.4 percent and African-Americans are just behind with 8 percent. American Indians make up less than 1 percent of Los Angeles' population.

Of course, there was a time, hundreds, or even thousands, of years ago, when American Indians made up the *entire* population of the area. Many different tribes lived along the Southern California coast, and it has been said that these first Californians spoke a greater number of languages than all the other inhabitants of the continent combined.

In 1542 Juan Rodriguez Cabrillo arrived in California and immediately noticed that a brown haze hung over the city caused by all of the Indians' fires. A little smog didn't seem to be that much of a problem 450 years ago, and it didn't discourage an ever-increasing number of Spanish explorers from coming to see this harsh paradise by the sea.

In 1769 an expedition under Gaspar de Portola came north from Mexico to explore the area all the way up to Monterey Bay. A Franciscan missionary named Juan Crespi kept a diary of the journey; it's the earliest surviving written record of Los Angeles' early days and of the first interaction between Indians and Hispanics. "Indeed, these heathen fold have pleased us a great deal," Crespi wrote, "having been (as they have) spending the whole day sitting with us, entirely without weapons or fear, as though they had been dealing with us forever."

Other Europeans began arriving with increasing frequency, but through the early 1800s, the Spanish continued to control Los Angeles. But after Texas was wrested away from Mexico in 1836 and became a state less than a decade later, the writing was on the wall for California. The United States' concept of Manifest Destiny meant that the entire North American continent should be a single nation under one government.

In 1846, led by Captain John Charles Fremont and Commander Robert F. Stockton, the United States Army took over Los Angeles; from that point on, L.A.—for better or worse—was an American city. The Americans brought an urgent sense of industry and progress to the area; but they brought violence, too. On one particularly shameful occasion, on October 26, 1871, a race riot broke out in Chinatown, leaving nineteen Chinese dead and the neighborhood looted and burned to the ground.

For all its variety of ethnicity, Los Angeles has never really been a true melting pot. There has always been an element of racial tension, sometimes flaring up in the horrors of the Watts Riots in 1966 or the L.A. riots in the wake of the Rodney King verdict in 1991. Los Angeles is made up of neighborhoods that, in many ways, are defined by race. Worldway, Watts, Compton, and Crenshaw are overwhelmingly Black. East L.A., Boyle Heights, Huntington Park, and Lincoln Heights are, by the great majority, Hispanic sections. Silver Lake and Westlake are predominantly Asian communities. And neighborhoods which contain over ninety percent Caucasian residents include Manhattan Beach, La Mesa, Beverly Hills, Burbank, Studio City, Woodland Hills, and Pacific Palisades.

There are those in each of these neighborhoods who would prefer to interact only with people of their own color and background. But for the rest of us, Los Angeles' multiculturalism is one of the keys to its excitement and life and diversity. In a way, it's like having the whole world concentrated into one sprawling area. Sure there are whites, blacks, Hispanics, and Asians as there are in most big American cities. But there are also Samoans, Aleuts, and Eskimos.

In fact, there must be at least two of every kind of person you can think of; it's like a giant Noah's Ark, except with plenty of oranges.

## Chapter X

# Culture? In L.A.?

As you're elbowing your way down Melrose Avenue, hoping that the sharp decorative object sticking through the fleshy part of someone's nose doesn't poke your eye out, you may be forgiven for wondering if Los Angeles is really the last word in Western Culture.

But, as this book shows, Los Angeles is nothing if not diverse. Wandering around town on a balmy evening, seeking the local art scene, you may encounter on one block raucous hooligans who have received an NEA grant to create an introspective sculpture on the theme of brotherly love made entirely out of rabbit entrails. On the next you'll find yourself cheek to jowl with tuxedo-clad sophisticates discussing the opera they have just seen and wondering aloud if anyone has already bought the sit-com rights to it. And further on you can sip bad wine and nibble worse cheese at the under-attended gallery retrospective of some great, neglected nineteenth-century photographer who specialized in taking pictures of under-attended galleries.

In short, Los Angeles has more diverse culture than a petri dish. (Did I hear a rim shot? Thank you.) You can hear symphony concerts, enjoy great live theater productions, and gaze upon some of the masterpieces of art from the entire span of human history, if that's your idea of a good time.

The following listing can't even pretend to be comprehensive. New art galleries open every day of the week at about the same rate that others close their doors. The city's museums are a little more permanent, but even they have explosive moments of flux (see, for instance, the Getty Museum which is one place as I write this and will be somewhere else by the time you read it).

But this chapter is a good starting place for you culture hounds. Whether you want to bask in the beauty of Impressionists in the Los Angeles County Museum of Art (LACMA) or be confronted by some striking, and sometimes disturbing, new art in a Melrose gallery like La Luz de Jesus, this line-up should offer you more than enough options.

And do yourself a favor. If you find a museum, gallery, or theater listed here that makes you think, "I'd never set foot in a place like that in a million years," consider going there. That's one of the more positive aspects of life in L.A.: no matter what you think or like, there's always an opposing viewpoint somewhere. The fun is in finding out what and where they are and in seeing how much they can change you.

But if you start to go too wild on Melrose, just remember: you're going to have that dragon tattoo on your inner thigh for the rest of your life, so think twice.

✉

In the case of the museums especially, it's best to call first to get information on pricing, parking, and current exhibits. An excellent monthly guide to the Los Angeles art happenings can be found in *ArtScene*. It's available for free at most galleries, but if you have trouble locating an issue, write *ArtScene* P.O. Box 861176, Los Angeles, CA 90086 or call (213) 482-4724.

# Art Museums

L.A. County Museum of Art
5905 Wilshire Boulevard    (213) 857-6000

LACMA is the big cahuna of Los Angeles art museums. Art lovers of just about every stripe should find something satisfying here, from a truly staggering collection of Japanese art to a recent retrospective of works from the Mayans to a fascinating permanent costume collection. The complex consists of five wings around an open courtyard. The exhibit rooms are gener-

ally spacious and well appointed, conducive to serious study or just a pleasant Sunday afternoon stroll among the canvases.

LACMA is just down the street from the La Brea Tar Pits, a necessary stop for any tourist or new-comer to Los Angeles (if you see a huge woolly mammoth stuck waist deep in a huge pool of tar, you've probably come to the right place). The Pits serve as both an interesting jaunt into history and a cautionary tale: whenever Hollywood types get too uppity, they would do well to gaze on some of the former movers and shakers in the area, now mired in stinky black goo.

Museum of Contemporary Art
250 S. Grand Avenue    (213) 626-6222

Art aficionados who, when confronted with the Old
Masters, sneer, "Seen it. Done it," are likely to prefer
MOCA to LACMA. This is the place to go when your
innermost soul needs modern, abstract art from bold
fellas like Rothko, Rauschenburg, and Warhol. For a
while, when LACMA was being built in 1984 (it was
designed by Arata Isozaki), the collection was housed
in a temporary museum in an old Los Angeles Police
Department garage. But the temporary quarters didn't
prove so temporary: today, both spaces are in use.


J. Paul Getty Museum
17985 Pacific Coast Highway, Malibu    (310) 459-7611

As you drive up and down the 405, just north of
Sunset Boulevard, you'll notice massive construction
going on; chances are you'll notice because it will have
stopped traffic for one reason or another. This is the
Getty Center in progress. When this multimillion dollar
complex is completed, it will house the massive collection
of art, photographs, and sculpture that now resides in the
far more modest J. Paul Getty Museum, an Italian-style
villa in Malibu. The collection contains a magnificent
photography collection and is particularly rich in Greek
and Roman antiquities. The building itself is also quite
beautiful; that new place up in Brentwood has its work
cut out for it in creating as warm and lovely a space to
commune with the art of centuries past.

Huntington Library, Art Collections, and Botanical
Gardens
1151 Oxford Street, San Marino    (818) 405-2141

You can have a wonderful aesthetic experience here
without ever going indoors. Sure, inside you can look at
Gainesborough's Blue Boy or look through the vast docu-
ments collection by and about Abraham Lincoln, but the
grounds of this magnificent 207-acre estate are worth a
visit all by themselves. Come at tea time and you can
enjoy a truly memorable high tea in one of the loveliest
settings imaginable.

The Autry Museum of Western Heritage
4700 Western Heritage Way, Griffith Park
(213) 667-2000

When you enter the courtyard you're greeted by a
large bronze statue of Gene Autry, strumming a guitar.
Inside you'll find a mix of fascinating Western exhibits
ranging from authentic weapons and wardrobes used by
the men and women who won the West to wonderful
memorabilia relating to movie and television cowboys:
Gene, Roy Rogers, John Wayne and just about everybody
else you can think of. Special exhibits highlight little-
known aspects of the Western experience, such as a recent
examination of Russian immigrants on the plains or a
thorough retrospective on the enduring image of Zorro.
The complex also houses a movie theater where Westerns
are shown every weekend.

Norton Simon Museum
411 W. Colorado Boulevard, Pasadena    (818) 449-6840

   For some reason this great museum is not as well
known as some of its big city cousins in Los Angeles, but
its magnificent collection marks it as one of the best
museums in the country. There are important works by
Picasso, Rembrandt, van Gogh, Reubens, Goya, Cezanne,
Renoir, Klee and many other masters, as well as a striking
collection of Asian sculpture and other artworks.

# Other Notable L.A. Museums

Museum of Neon Art
154 Universal City Walk    (213) 617-1580

Armand Hammer Museum of Art
10889 Wilshire Boulevard    (310) 443-7020

Long Beach Museum of Art
2300 Ocean Boulevard, Long Beach    (310) 439-2119

California Museum of Afro-American History
and Culture
600 State Drive    (213) 744-7432

Santa Monica Museum of Art
2437 Main Street    (310) 399-0433

California Museum of Photography
3824 Main Street, Downtown Pedestrian Mall, Riverside
(909) 784-FOTO

# Art Galleries

Handmade Galleries
14556 Ventura Boulevard, Sherman Oaks
(818) 382-3444
Intriguing collection of hand-crafted artwork ranging from pottery to clothing to jewelry to painting to toys to furniture. The artists are often on hand to answer questions about their work—and to accept commissions for custom-made art.

La Luz de Jesus
7400 Melrose (upstairs from The Soap Plant, a great, funky gift and book shop)   (213) 651-4875
Contemporary folk art, with an emphasis on "Day of the Dead" creations.

Northlight Gallery
10850 W. Pico Boulevard, #404 (at Westside Pavilion)
(310) 441-1923
Original contemporary art, from oils and watercolors to sculpture and photography.

Municipal Art Gallery
4804 Hollywood Boulevard   (213) 485-4581
Contemporary Southern California artists.

Institution of Creative Art
7080 Hollywood Boulevard, Suite 321   (213) 962-9879
Spanish and international fine art.

Ace Gallery
5514 Wilshire Boulevard   (213) 935-4411
Original contemporary art.

Gallery of Functional Art
2429 Main Street, Santa Monica   (310) 450-2827
Artsy furniture.

Fahey-Klein Gallery
148 N. La Brea Avenue    (213) 934-2250
Contemporary photography.

The Folk Tree
217 S. Fair Oaks Avenue, Pasadena    (818) 795-8733
The Folk Tree Collection, 199 S. Fair Oaks Avenue,
Pasadena    (818) 793-4828
Mexican folk art: jewelry, clothing, toys, books, sculpture.

# Live Theater

Let's not kid ourselves. Los Angeles is a movie town
the way Detroit is a car town. But even in the Motor City
you can find a few hardy souls riding bicycles. And even
in Hollywood, there are still places where real live people
can watch other real live people stand on a stage and act.
L.A. can't compete with real theater towns like New York,
but there's a surprisingly varied theatrical life in this
movie town—and varied places in which to experience it.

The big productions generally end up in places like
the Shubert Theater, 2020 Avenue of the Stars, Century
City (800) 447-7400. At this writing, *Cats* is playing at the
Shubert. And when you read this, it'll probably still be
there. Or some other big deal just like it.

Steve Martin's intellectual comedy *Picasso at the
Lapin Agile* enjoyed a profitable and critically acclaimed
run at the Westwood Playhouse, 10886 Le Conte Avenue, Westwood (310) 208-5454. And at this writing, a
minimalist production of *Hamlet* (no costumes, sets, or
props) is playing to minimal audiences (just kidding;
don't sue me) at L.A. Theatre Center, 516 S. Spring Street
(213) 485-1681.

The Mark Taper Forum, 135 N. Grand Avenue (213) 365-3500 is a fine venue for larger productions, as is the Doolittle Theater, 1615 N. Vine Street (213) 365-3500.

If you have a taste for classical theater, Glendale's A Noise Within, 234 S. Brand Avenue (818) 546-1924, offers an intriguing variety. Not long ago, for instance, you could have chosen among Shakespeare's *King Lear*, Sheridan's *A School For Scandal*, and Steinbeck's *Of Mice and Men* playing in rotation.

Other notable and/or interesting Los Angeles area theaters include:

Ventura Court Theatre
12417 Ventura Court, Studio City   (213) 660-TKTS

The Open Fist Theatre
1625 N. La Brea Avenue   (213) 882-6912

Theatre West
3333 Cahuenga Boulevard   (213) 851-7977

Theatre/Theater
1713 North Cahuenga Boulevard   (213) 850-6941

Stella Adler Theatre
6773 Hollywood Boulevard   (213) 469-3942

The Gascon Center Theatre
8735 Washington Boulevard, Culver City
(213) 660-8587

The Doolittle Theatre
1615 N. Vine Street   (213) 365-3500

The Venue
600 Moulton Avenue   (213) 221-5894

Angels Theatre
2106 Hyperion Avenue, Silverlake   (213) 466-1767

The Audrey Skirball-Kenis Theatre
9070 Venice Boulevard   (310) 284-9027

Hudson Theatre
6539 Santa Monica Boulevard   (213) 660-8587

The Hudson Backstage
6539 Santa Monica Boulevard   (213) 462-0265

The New York Theatre
6468 Santa Monica Boulevard   (213) 466-1767

West Coast Ensemble
6240 Hollywood Boulevard   (213) 871-1052

Pantages Theater
6233 Hollywood Boulevard   (310) 410-1062

Pasadena Playhouse
39 S. Molino Avenue   (818) 356-7529

Ahmanson Theater
135 N. Grand Avenue   (213) 972-7211

Coronet Theater
366 N. La Cienega Boulevard   (310) 657-7377

International City Theater
Long Beach City College, Clark Avenue and Harvey Way,
Long Beach   (310) 420-4128

## Concert Halls

Classical music isn't entirely unknown in Los
Angeles. In fact, it held an important place in the heart of
the city even before (believe it or not) movies came along.
Once the movies arrived, L.A. became a mecca for fine
musicians. First, they were needed to accompany silent
films in the wonderful orchestras that once had a home

in every major movie theater. Then, after the dawn of sound, every studio had excellent orchestras to provide the rich and rewarding musical scores for thousands of motion pictures.

Today, some of the greatest classical musicians regularly perform in Los Angeles. Following are a few of the better-known haunts for longhair music, but when you get into town, check your local listings.

The Los Angeles Philharmonic, one of the nation's finest orchestras, often appears at the Dorothy Chandler Pavilion, 135 N. Grand Avenue (213) 365-3500. The Dorothy Chandler also regularly offers opera and other theatrical productions. Not to mention the Academy Awards (oh, but we were discussing culture, weren't we?).

The Ambassador Auditorium, 300 W. Green Street in Pasadena (800) CONCERT is also an excellent venue for everything from concerts by symphony orchestras to intimate piano recitals. So is Center Theater at the Long Beach Convention Center, 300 E. Ocean Boulevard (310) 596-5556, home of the Long Beach Opera.

The Bing Auditorium at the Los Angeles County Museum of Art (see address above) is a kind of all-purpose theater, sometimes showing films and other times offering excellent chamber or solo concerts. And the Harriet and Charles Luckman Fine Arts Complex, Cal State L.A. (213) 466-1767, regularly offers not only excellent classical music, but a variety of dance presentations, too.

But most Angelenos, God bless 'em, have one favorite place in which to enjoy classical music: the Hollywood Bowl, 2301 N. Highland Avenue (213) 480-3232. For decades, the Bowl has been L.A.'s cultural mainstay. The great orchestras and artists of the world have played in the huge outdoor shell. Because of the nature of the place—it's as big as all outdoors—the Bowl can offer musical events of a magnitude that can't be equaled anywhere else in town. Recently, the Japan American Symphony performed Beethoven's *Ninth Symphony* (called *Daiku* in Japan) with a chorus of 1,000 singers— 500 Japanese, 500 American. And it's a tribute to the love which Angelenos have for classical music (and a good spectacle) that the audience always outnumbers the performers.

## Chapter XI

# No Thanks, I'm Just Looking: Shopping in L.A.

When it comes to tossing the green around, citizens of Los Angeles have a certain reputation. Watching movies like *Pretty Woman* or television shows like *Beverly Hills 90210*, the rest of the country can live vicariously through dangerously beautiful people with no credit limit on their Visa cards who live to shop and shop to live.

The sad truth is that most people who live in Los Angeles are just regular Joes like you and me (well, you anyway) who clip coupons and shop at Target and IKEA and look forward to after-Christmas sales when prices are slashed to the bone.

But the fantasy of Beverly Hills shopping is not just the stuff of movies. There really are, you will be shocked to learn, people who can and will stroll into a shop and drop a cool thousand bucks on a shirt you wouldn't be found dead in a ditch in. They may not light cigars with fifty-dollar bills anymore, but that's only because nobody in Los Angeles smokes. This is a town in which a few people have way too much of the money, and I'll resent it and fight it until I'm one of 'em.

The center of Beverly Hills' shopping universe is Rodeo Drive, fabled in song and story and *Tonight Show* monologues. This slightly dowdy and unprepossessing little street connects Wilshire Boulevard and Santa Monica Boulevard. If you drive along Rodeo (and you will, believe me, you will), you won't find much of its famed glitter and dash making itself obvious to you. For that, you actually have to park the car and walk into one of the shops. When you do, you might want to have your spouse take a picture of your face the first time you get a load of the price tag on a pair of artfully torn, faded, and shrunken jeans. Trust me, your expression will be good for a lot of laughs when you get back home.

But perhaps the greatest proof of Rodeo Drive's exclusivity is that you can't even walk into some of the stores. You have to make an appointment. Maybe it's just me, but the thought of someone making an appointment to go into a store to spend more than I spent on my car to buy  a mink sweater vest is proof enough that we are about a hop, skip, and a jump away from the Apocalypse.

However, if you have roughly eight times the value of your home burning a hole in your pocket, you might find a visit to Cartier's, Giorgio Armani's, Hammacher Schlemmer's, or Bijan (that's one of the places that requires a reservation) to be just what the doctor ordered.

A stroll along Melrose Avenue will provide you with a shopping experience that has very little in common with what you just experienced on Rodeo. Melrose is lined with funky shops offering clothes, books, gifts, and food. There are art galleries, antique shops, furniture stores, and theaters. Everything on Melrose is tinged with attitude, but you can actually come home with some unique treasures and still have enough left in the bank to make at least part of the rent.

Of course, Los Angeles virtually invented Mall Culture. The Sherman Oaks Galleria, at Sepulveda and Ventura Boulevard in Sherman Oaks, is the archetypal mall; it's the place that gave the world that priceless treasure, the Valley Girl. Beverly Center on Beverly Drive in Beverly Hills (is this getting redundant or is it just me?) is also a fine mall with a great variety of shops and restaurants. But when push comes to shove, all malls everywhere are pretty much the same. If you're coming in from out of town, you might want to visit the Sherman Oaks Galleria just to hear if anyone will say "Grody to the max" or "Gag me with a spoon" or other historic phrases. Otherwise, you're better off shopping further down Ventura Boulevard where there are galleries and bookstores aplenty.

I dragged my wife kicking and screaming to Los Angeles from Boston, and she still misses having great walking/shopping neighborhoods like Harvard Square or Newberry Street. We've only found a few suitable replacements. One is Westwood Village, a pleasant neighborhood close to UCLA where you can park the car, then have a meal, browse through a bookstore, catch a movie, get coffee and dessert, all without getting into your car again. Only longtime Angelenos can appreciate how rare that is.

Another nice walking neighborhood is found on San Fernando Road in Burbank just next to the huge Media Center Mall. San Fernando Road is getting a little bland these days, as more and more of the original shops are leaving and being replaced by the omnipresent Starbucks Coffee and Blockbuster Video, but there are still a number of good bookstores, magazine stands, hobby shops, and general merchandise stores of all descriptions. One particularly interesting store is Movie World, which offers books on all aspects of the movies, as well as posters and stills and magazines and other memorabilia. It's crowded and kind of dusty—just like a real bookstore should be.

If neither of those neighborhoods fit your shopping criteria, try the Third Street Promenade in Santa Monica. Only a few blocks from the beach, this street has been closed off to traffic, creating an open-air mall. The street is rife with excellent antique shops, art galleries, and antiquarian bookstores. There's a particularly festive atmosphere on the Promenade on weekends. Even if you don't buy anything, you're apt to have a thoroughly pleasant day. Try saying that about Rodeo Drive.

## Chapter XII

# Restaurants and Night Spots

For a place where so many thin people live, Los Angeles sure is crawling with restaurants, cafes, diners, greasy spoons, pizza dives, and doughnut shops. A lot of business—maybe *most* business—is conducted over a meal. You've heard the phrase, "Let's do lunch." That really means, "Let's pretend to eat lunch, but actually have a business meeting over chips and salsa." I've often wondered how many life-altering deals never got made because some poor chump actually thought he was having lunch and ordered a big, sloppy barbecue sandwich, which then splattered bright red, spicy sauce over every whereas and hereto in the contract.

Restaurants in L.A. are also places to see and be seen (also a good reason not to order the barbecue). Star-gazers will always have the best luck in spotting their prey in a restaurant—and not a fancy, expensive Spago kind of place, either. I've seen big-time celebrities in Bob's Big Boy and Papoo's hot dog joint in Toluca Lake; at a cheap Mexican restaurant in Burbank; and in each of the holy trinity of Valley delis: Solley's, Art's, and Jerry's.

Talk to old-timers about their most memorable Hollywood moments and, inevitably, they'll tell you about a private supper at the Brown Derby or the time they met Chaplin at Musso and Frank's or the night they went slumming for a bowl of chili at Barney's Beanery.

Restaurants have always been the life blood of Los Angeles, still are, and always will be. In this chapter I'll discuss some of the great ones that have already disappeared, a few legendary haunts that are still suffused with the slightly musty glamour of an earlier time, and maybe even a few relatively new kids on the block. They're each worth a visit for one reason or another. In some, the atmosphere is the most important thing and you'll just have to put up with the food. In others, you'll just shrug, say "Atmosphere, schmatmosphere," and eat like a pig.

In all of them, you're pretty likely to see someone you recognize. Here are the rules: 1. Don't gawk; 2. Don't ask for an autograph while someone is eating; 3. Don't bring your barbecue sandwich over to the celebrity's table and ask if he wants a bite. Beyond that, have a ball.

And save room for dessert.

## Musso and Frank

6667 Hollywood Boulevard

A diligent scholar, when researching this particular restaurant, immediately runs head-on into a brick wall on the unlikeliest of subjects, i.e., exactly what is the name of this place? The sign on the building reads "Musso and Frank." But surviving photographs from the twenties and thirties reveal that the name above the door is "Musso and Franks." In ninety percent of literature about Hollywood restaurants, it is referred to as "Musso and Frank's."

Last time I was there, in between bites of a New York strip steak, done just so, I asked a few of the waiters (who have worked there since dinosaurs walked the earth) about the name. No one knew. And no one cared. "Anyway," one of them pointed out, "most people just called it 'Musso's.'"

No matter what you call it, every Hollywood veteran has eaten there—it's the oldest restaurant in town—and it continues to be a great place for old-fashioned, no-nonsense, meat-and-potato meals. Musso's was built at 6669 Hollywood Boulevard in 1919 by Frank Toulet and John Musso, and they ran it for a few years until they sold it to (what are the odds?) John Mosso and Joseph Carisimi. In 1936 a new room was built next door at 6667 Hollywood Boulevard.

From the beginning Musso's was a casual hangout for the stars; it didn't demand the putting-on-the-ritz glamour of some of the more glittery nightspots, and the food was unpretentious and generally inexpensive. Musso's also has, for those whose tastes run that way, a beautiful and well-appointed bar. It's still a good place to spot stars, too, but the deep, circular booths help to ensure everyone's privacy.

But the most impressive celebrities in Musso and Frank are not those there in the flesh, but those whose former presence helps to give the place such a sense of the past: Charlie Chaplin used to hang out here. So did Orson Welles and writers like Hemingway, Faulkner, and Nathanael West (did I mention the place has a great bar?). Everything about Musso and Frank evokes an earlier period in Hollywood history. Just outside, Hollywood Boulevard is nothing like the street of dreams that tourists expect, but once you've stepped inside to the oak and leather ambience of Musso's, suddenly the Golden Age is back.

# Brown Derby

1628 North Vine Street
*The "Hat" Brown Derby*
3427 Wilshire Boulevard

When Herbert Somborn decided, in 1926, to open a
new restaurant on Wilshire Boulevard, across from the
Ambassador Hotel, he gave a great deal of thought to the
menu and atmosphere. But he didn't give two hoots about
its name. "You could open a restaurant in an alley and call
it anything," he said. "If the food and service were good,
the patrons would just come flocking. It could even be
called something as ridiculous as the Brown Derby."

So the Brown Derby it was, and to drive the name
home the place was designed to look like, well, a big hat.
Although intended as a first-class restaurant (former
Ziegfeld Follies girls were hired as waitresses), the Brown
Derby was actually a kind of glorified diner. The wall
of the round room was lined with comfortable booths,
each lit with a lamp shaped like a little derby. The menu
consisted of popular fare like corned beef hash and
pot roast, and the waitresses wore derby-shaped hoop-
skirts.

The Brown Derby quickly became a popular Holly-
wood hangout, serving regulars like John Barrymore,
Douglas Fairbanks, W.C. Fields, and Mae Murray. Famed
Hollywood wit and sometime screenwriter Wilson Mizner
once slugged it out with John Gilbert in the Brown Derby.
In those days, there was glamour and excitement in
Hollywood, on and off the screen. Or does it just seem
that way to us in the decidedly unglamorous nineties?

The Brown Derby was so successful that on Valen-
tine's Day 1929, a second restaurant with the same name
was opened on Vine Street. This one was, if anything,
even more popular than the first. The walls were lined

*The Brown Derby in the twenties*

with celebrity caricatures, and every table was equipped with a telephone connection—a Hollywood first. The new Derby offered the same simple menu as the old, but the presence of a maitre d' and a crack staff of immaculately dressed waiters gave the place a real upscale sheen.

The Vine Street Brown Derby closed in 1985, and the building was destroyed by fire a couple of years later. The Wilshire Derby survives still, in a manner of speaking. It was about to be torn down by developers when anxious conservationists protested. They reached a compromise. The old derby-shaped building now sits, at approximately its old Wilshire Boulevard address, atop a mini-mall.

# Formosa Cafe

7156 Santa Monica Boulevard

Musso and Frank offers an atmosphere of Holly-wood's past and so does, in a different way, the seedy Formosa Cafe. Lined with photographs of movie stars, the walls fairly reek of the past. Even at midday the Formosa is dark and slightly clammy. In fact, local legend has it that the ghost of a famous movie star (exactly *which* famous movie star is something that few agree on) walks through the low-ceilinged rooms of the Formosa (the place was actually built from an old red car from the abandoned Los Angeles trolley system).

Built across the street from Warner Hollywood studio, formerly the Goldwyn Studios, the Formosa was once a very popular lunchtime hangout with movie people, both those in front of and behind the camera. These days, its bar remains pretty popular at night, but you'll never have trouble getting a lunch table. The food is better than you might expect, but the Formosa isn't a place to go to eat. You go there to soak up the slightly rancid atmosphere of the days when the people in all those photos on the wall actually came here themselves, grabbing a quick bite, or a drink or two, before getting back to the business of creating movie classics.

You might want to put a visit to the Formosa Cafe at the top of your list, since it always seems in imminent danger of being torn down. Currently, it looks like the Cafe is merely going to be moved, but nothing is perma-nent in Hollywood, not even a place where Tinseltown ghosts walk.

# Barney's Beanery

8447 Santa Monica Boulevard

Today this place looks a lot like a biker bar, filled with rock 'n' rollers and street people with style (sometimes) and attitude (always). If you feel like you're slumming when you go there, then you're just part of Barney's grand tradition; it's always been a place for slumming. Stars like Jean Harlow used to hang out here in the thirties, and it was particularly popular among the rough-and-tumble directors like Howard Hawks and Wild Bill Wellman. Barney's Beanery is famous for its incredible selection of beers. And if you like ribs and chili and other forms of hash-house cuisine, you'll have a grand time at Barney's. It's a loud, raucous place; at once a relic of Hollywood's deepest past and a cutting edge meeting place for the new kids in town.

# Spago

1114 Van Horn

Wanna see movie stars? This is the place. Simply lie about who you are in order to get a table, and mortgage your house to pay for the meal, and you can stare at the biggest names in show biz till the cows come home. The cuisine by chef/owner Wolfgang Puck is considered to be among the finest in the area. To future Hollywood historians, the star-studded Spago will be as important to this generation as the Cocoanut Grove or the Brown Derby were to the stars of the thirties and forties. Present Hollywood historians can't afford to eat there.

# The Cafe Trocadero
8610 Sunset Boulevard

# The Mocambo
8588 Sunset Boulevard

# Ciro's

8433 Sunset Boulevard

In the thirties and forties, if you were looking for a good time on the Sunset Strip, you had your choice of three terrific nightspots: the Cafe Trocadero, the Mocambo, and Ciro's. Today, they're all gone, leaving behind only memories of hundreds of exciting Hollywood nights.

The Cafe Trocadero opened in 1934. Its opening night party was a private bash, hosted by super agent Myron Selznick, brother of producer David O. Selznick. The guest list included Bing Crosby, Dorothy Parker, Fred Astaire, Sam Goldwyn, Myrna Loy, William Wellman, Ida Lupino, Jeanette MacDonald, Gilbert Roland, and a host of other Hollywood big shots. The official opening came on September 17 with a formal dinner-dance. The Hollywood crowd never cared how much money they threw around, so nobody complained aloud that it cost $7.50 *per person*! for the festivities. The Cafe Trocadero, writes Jim Heiman in his book *Out With the Stars*, "virtually ushered in Hollywood's golden age of glamour. The Trocadero became the focal point in town to see and be seen, the stars' idea of a perfect nightclub."

The Cafe Trocadero closed its doors in 1946. Today, only the three steps that led up to the front door survive.

When the Mocambo opened its doors on January 3, 1941, it stole some of the Trocadero's thunder. The interior was baroque, to the point of being bizarre; the club's

*Ciro's in the fifties*

centerpiece was a huge aviary, filled with parakeets, love birds, macaws, and a cockatoo. The place cost $100,000 to build and patrons gladly paid $10 apiece to get in; big money for 1941. But who wouldn't shell out ten bucks for the chance to rub elbows with Lana Turner, Cary Grant, Hedy LaMarr, Cole Porter, Irving Berlin, Marlene Dietrich, Judy Garland, Henry Fonda, James Stewart, or any of the others of the scores of celebrities who came to the Mocambo for a good time?

The Mocambo flourished until 1958, when changing times finally tarnished its glamour. The site is now the parking lot of the Playboy Building on the Sunset Strip.

Just down the street, another flashy nightspot opened in January 1940. Ciro's was built by entrepreneur Billy

Wilkerson, who was also the man behind the Cafe Trocadero. For a time, it was the hottest spot in town, but within three years it was closed. It reopened under new management and—helped along by entertainment by Dean Martin, Jerry Lewis, Sophie Tucker, Sammy Davis Jr., Peggy Lee, Maurice Chevalier, Liberace, and others— Ciro's became the place to be, once again. Ciro's closed down in 1957. The barely recognizable building now houses the Comedy Store, that premiere showcase for standup comedy, owned by Mitzi Shore.

## Chasen's

9039 Beverly Boulevard

One of the most famous and elegant of the old-time Hollywood nightspots, Chasen's began life on December 13, 1936 as the Southern Pit Barbecue. There were six tables, a counter with eight stools, and a bar with six stools. Chili was sold at a quarter a bowl, and ribs were served up for thirty-five cents. The drinks were cheap, too, and pretty soon the Southern Pit was crawling with celebrities ranging from James Cagney to W.C. Fields (did someone say cheap drinks?) to Buddy Ebsen. Owner Dave Chasen gradually transformed the place into a real restaurant with a full menu. It was here that Shirley Temple insisted on having a drink like her parents were enjoying. So the bartender whipped up a sweet blend of grenadine, ginger ale, and fruit and gave it to the little star. She liked it and so did generations of kids to come who would order a "Shirley Temple."

Chasen's was also a remarkably accommodating place. When Dorothy Lamour, quite pregnant, was uncomfortable at table 12, Dave Chasen had a section cut out so that she could breathe more easily.

But Chasen's never got so fancy that it ceased making the chili on which its fame was founded. When a celebrity was admitted to Cedars-Sinai Medical Center, Chasen's would ship over some chili so they wouldn't have to suffer with hospital food; ulcer patients must have been particularly grateful. During the production of *Cleopatra* in 1961, Elizabeth Taylor missed Chasen's chili so much that she had it flown over to Italy on a regular basis.

Chasen's was, through the years, among the most formal of Hollywood eateries; men had to wear ties and reservations were essential. Perhaps because today's Hollywood is a far more casual place, Chasen's began to lose favor. In 1994 the property was sold to developer Ira Smedra who intended to demolish the place and then erect a mall on the property with a supermarket, a chain drugstore, and, maybe, a scaled-down version of the very restaurant that is being torn down to make way for this new enterprise.

There was even a report in *The Los Angeles Times*, January 13, 1995, that Spago owner Wolfgang Puck wanted to turn the restaurant into one of his cafes which "offer diluted versions of his Spago dishes." Puck, however, assured the *Times*, "I haven't signed anything. It's not even around the corner. They still have to tear it down and then they have to build it." No matter what happens, the restaurant that opens in Chasen's former location won't really be Chasen's. That venerable old bit of Hollywood class is irreplaceable.

Chasen's closed its doors on April 1, 1995. A friend and I had lunch there a few days earlier, the day after the restaurant's final Oscar bash, attended by Robert de Niro, Danny Devito, Quentin Tarentino, and other major celebrities. Things had been crazy there the night before, but that Tuesday lunchtime was quiet and pleasant. We were able to enjoy a bowl of the famous chili, talk about this and that, and look for movie stars (we didn't see any).

Mostly, we just wanted to soak in the atmosphere, for the last time, an atmosphere still redolent of the days when Clark Gable, W.C. Fields, Barbara Stanwyck, the Barrymores, Howard Hughes, and every U.S. President since Eisenhower used the place as their hangout.

When we stepped out into the brilliant sunlight of the March afternoon, it was like being snatched out of the past into a harsher present. We had lunched at Chasen's and we knew that we could never, ever do it again.

When Chasen's went, the last of elegant Golden Age Hollywood dining went with it.

## Thelma Todd's Sidewalk Cafe

17575 Pacific Coast Highway

The beautiful mission-style building that faces the Pacific Ocean is today used by Paulist Fathers for a television production center. But in the thirties, it was the site of a spectacular, short-lived nightspot that was touched liberally with both glamour and tragedy. It was owned by actress Thelma Todd, the beautiful "ice cream blonde" comedienne who often appeared in the films of the Marx Brothers and Laurel and Hardy. She and film director Roland West had opened the Cafe in 1934, where it immediately became renowned, in the words of one writer, "as *the* expense account restaurant in the area. In the depths of the Depression, those who could afford Thelma Todd's Sidewalk Cafe were paying $50 for lunch!" One principal attraction seems to have been the private dining areas. These little rooms were popular with movie executives who wanted to have a quiet lunch with a promising young starlet; the kind of thing a wife might misunderstand—as though any such thing would ever happen in Hollywood.

After Thelma Todd's death [see Chapter VII, "Unsolved L.A. Mysteries"], Roland West continued to operate the cafe, but it never really caught on. Its Malibu location might have been a tad remote. It may also be that the aura of tragedy that surrounded the place was not titillating, as it sometimes is, but only depressing.

## The Players

8225 Sunset Boulevard

In August 1938 writer/director Preston Sturges (*The Lady Eve*, *The Miracle of Morgan's Creek*, *The Palm Beach Story*) bought a house on the Sunset Strip which had once belonged to silent comedy star Chester Conklin. It had been, Sturges wrote in his autobiography, "converted by a later owner into the Hollywood Wedding Chapel. I didn't have any immediate plans for the property, but its site was a marvelous location for a theater, a club...almost anything."

*The Player's Restaurant*

The "almost anything" turned out to be a nightclub/ restaurant called The Players, a place as lively and eccentric as the man who created it. The Players opened in the summer of 1940, and in no time, Sturges wrote, it had "attracted on a regular basis not only the celebrated producers, directors, writers, stars, and agents of Hollywood, but visiting admirals and generals and potentates and old Texas spenders on double-ended benders and the tourists who wanted to see them all."

For those who got in, The Players was a wonderful place. The trouble is, you never knew whether you could get in or not. If Sturges felt like having a private soiree for a few friends, he simply closed The Players' doors and had a ball. Perhaps as a result, the place failed after the first year. Sturges rethought things and added on The Playroom, a restaurant/nightclub. On the top floor he built a small theater. Howard Hughes, Barbara Stanwyck, Orson Welles, and Humphrey Bogart were regulars, the food was superb, and the atmosphere was a heady combination of wild hilarity and casual sophistication—not unlike a Preston Sturges film.

The Players, however, continued to lose money. Even some well-received productions of comedies like *Room Service* in the upstairs theater failed to bring in enough money to justify Sturges' four mortgages on the place. In 1952 he lost The Players to the Internal Revenue Service. His film career was also in sharp decline, and within a few years one of Hollywood's most brilliant creators was virtually forgotten.

Happily, Sturges is today considered a true filmmaking genius. But only a few old-timers now remember the rollicking, eccentric nightclub that Preston Sturges owned and where he and his friends once ruled the roost.

# Chapter XIII

# Cemeteries

There are many, many people, I've found, who love cemeteries and enjoy spending time in them. And there are just as many people who can't for the life of them figure out why. I am one of the first group. I've been fascinated by cemeteries for as long as I can remember. They appeal to the historian in me. Deeper down, cemeteries speak to my very heart and soul, connecting me with the past and all its citizens who sleep in those peaceful spots. Some find cemeteries morbid, but I find them oddly comforting. When faced with my all-too-human fear of mortality, a contemplative stroll around a cemetery helps put things in perspective. "Heck," I think. "All *these* people died. How bad can it be?"

In Los Angeles, of course, there is an added attraction to the many cemeteries that dot the landscape: star power. I'll never get to meet Marilyn Monroe or W.C. Fields or John Barrymore or Fred Astaire. But I can visit with them nonetheless and ponder the simplicity of Monroe's mausoleum slot against the epic grandeur of Barrymore's monument, complete with reflecting pool.

As with all cities, a visit to any of Los Angeles' cemeteries is both history lesson and celebration. These

memorial parks are poignant, beautiful, sometimes
funny, sometimes depressing, often downright weird—
not unlike Los Angeles itself.

# Forest Lawn Glendale

1712 South Glendale Avenue

With its lovely, rolling landscape, ornate statuary,
and impressive roster of, um, permanent residents,
Glendale's Forest Lawn is probably *the* cemetery to visit
if you can visit only one. L. Frank Baum, the author of
*The Wizard of Oz*, is buried there, as is another great
author from the opposite end of the style spectrum,
Theodore Dreiser. Cowboy hero Tom Mix, opera star
Lawrence Tibbett, evangelists Kathryn Kuhlman and
Aimee Semple MacPherson (rumor has it that she was
buried with a live phone in her coffin, so she could give
the living a ring if something occurred to her), singers
Sam Cooke and Nat "King" Cole, all-around entertainer
Sammy Davis Jr., and gruff baseball manager Casey
Stengel are there, too.

The list of movie legends at Glendale's Forest Lawn
ranges from the sublime (Mary Pickford, Ethel Waters,
Clara Bow, Jean Harlow, Jeannette MacDonald, Carole
Lombard, Clark Gable, Walt Disney, Errol Flynn, Spencer
Tracy) to the ridiculous (Chico and Gummo Marx, Larry
Fine of the Three Stooges) to the sublimely ridiculous
(Gracie Allen, Theda Bara).

You can also find the last resting places of dramatist
Clifford Odets, singer Russ Columbo, actors Alan Ladd,
Robert Taylor, and Francis X. Bushman, producers David
O. Selznick and Irving Thalberg, and wide-mouthed
comic Joe E. Brown.

# Forest Lawn Hollywood Hills

6300 Forest Lawn Drive

In the hills overlooking the Warner Bros., NBC, and Disney Studios in Burbank, Forest Lawn offers some much-needed perspective to the egomaniacal producers and performers who work in its shadow. Not that it works; show biz egos need more deflating than a simple idea like the Transience of Life can provide.

The Hollywood Hills Forest Lawn has a sparser, more manicured look than its Glendale cousin. It also has an alert sales staff. If you tell them at the gate that you "just want to look around" they figure you're shopping for a plot. Just take the brochure and move on if you want to save time. Who knows? You might actually want to settle there once you see that your neighbors would include comic geniuses Buster Keaton, Lucille Ball, and Stan Laurel, actress Bette Davis, big game hunter Clyde Beatty, pioneer dancer Ruth St. Denis, classic Western sidekicks Smiley Burnette and Gabby Hayes, and pop-eyed comic Marty Feldman.

Actors George Raft and Charles Laughton are also interred here, as are bandleader Horace Heidt, band-leader-turned-television producer and actor Ozzie Nelson, film director Fritz Lang, flamboyant pianist Liberace, jazz musician Red Nichols, deadpan "Joe Friday" Jack Webb, and T.V. pioneer Ernie Kovacs. And let us not forget the greatest of all cartoon directors, Fred "Tex" Avery.

Hollywood Hills' Forest Lawn features, for reasons I can't quite fathom, a sixty-foot monument to George Washington and a replica of Boston's Old North Church.

# Mt. Sinai Memorial Park

5950 Forest Lawn Drive

This small cemetery, adjacent to Hollywood Hills' Forest Lawn, is worth a visit for its moving tributes to Hebrew history. The Memorial Monument, by sculptor Bernard Zakheim, is a powerful commemoration of those who died in the Holocaust. Nearby, The Heritage, a huge mosaic, 145 feet long, depicts important moments of the Jewish experience in America.

Comedian Phil Silvers is interred just to the right of the mural. Nearby are actors Lee J. Cobb, Billy Halop of "the Bowery Boys," Herschel Bernardi, and Hollywood columnist Sidney Skolsky.

# Hollywood Memorial

6000 Santa Monica Boulevard

There is something a little seedy and old-fashioned about Hollywood Memorial Park that makes it among the most evocative of area cemeteries; when you step onto the grounds it is though you have slipped back into the past. The grounds are lush, lovely, and secluded, and it's easy to forget that you are standing in the middle of a bustling urban area, in the shadow of several movie studios.

Many important (or notorious, or both) citizens of earlier Los Angeles lie in Hollywood Memorial Park: Colonel Griffith J. Griffith, who had donated 3,000 acres—later named Griffith Park—to the city; General Harrison Gray Otis, former editor of the *Los Angeles Times*; Harry Chandler, Otis' son-in-law and also the paper's editor; rancher John T. Gower; philanthropists

Frederick W. Blanchard and William A. Clark Jr.; gangster Benjamin "Bugsy" Siegel; author Gene Stratton Porter; and the couple who named Hollywood, Horace H. Wilcox and Daeida Wilcox Beveridge.

Two members of the beloved "Our Gang" troupe are interred here: Carl "Alfalfa" Switzer and Darla Hood. So are movie moguls Cecil B. De Mille, Harry Cohn, and Jess Lasky.

Silent movie legends are here in abundance: Douglas Fairbanks (in the park's most elaborate tomb, on a marble, pillared stage fronted by a long reflecting pool), Rudolph Valentino (in an unpretentious crypt with the family of a friend), Janet Gaynor, Renee Adoree, Barbara LaMarr, Marion Davies, and the famous Talmadge sisters, Norma, Constance, and Natalie. Hannah Chaplin, the mother of Charlie, is also buried here.

Some of the graves in Hollywood Memorial Park are reminders of Hollywood scandals and mysteries. Film director William Desmond Taylor's murder has never been solved. And when aspiring starlet Virginia Rappe died in 1921, comedian Roscoe "Fatty" Arbuckle was charged with her murder. Although later acquitted, his career was ruined. Next to Miss Rappe lies her lover, director Henry Lehrman, who reportedly visited her grave once a week until his own death in 1946.

Actors Peter Lorre, Clifton Webb, and Peter Finch are buried here. So is tap dancer Eleanor Powell and director Victor Fleming. Actress Joan Hackett has, perhaps, the most eye-catching epitaph: "Go away, I'm asleep."

# Holy Cross

5835 West Slauson Avenue

Holy Cross is a serene, lovely location, highlighted by a grotto with an altar and a statue of the Virgin Mary. It's a peaceful spot, but if some of Holy Cross' residents had gathered here in life, the joint would have been jumping. Just think of the jam session possible with Bing Crosby, pioneer jazz trombonist "Kid" Ory, conductor Jose Iturbi, dancer Ray Bolger, and that crazed purveyor of novelty tunes, Spike Jones.

You want laughs instead of music? Some of the greats rest at Holy Cross: Jimmy Durante, Joan Davis, Edgar Kennedy, Jack "the Tin Man" Haley, Jackie Coogan, and the King of Comedy, Mack Sennett.

Actors Pat O'Brien, Charles Boyer, Rita Hayworth, Rosalind Russell, Gene Lockhart, and Richard Arlen are buried here. So are some major figures from two very different tragedies: Sharon Tate and her unborn baby, both murdered by members of the Manson Family in 1969; and Evelyn Nesbit, over whom Harry K. Thaw murdered architect Stanford White in 1906.

Gossip columnist Louella Parsons lies here, not far from those troubled rich kids Gloria Vanderbilt (and her twin Thelma Furness) and Nicky Hilton, once married to Elizabeth Taylor. America's greatest film director, John Ford, is buried next to his wife Mary.

And, lest we forget, there is buried in this cemetery an actor who was known to crawl out of a coffin on a regular basis: Bela Lugosi. Lugosi's career went progressively downhill in the last years of his life, but he retained a certain panache, even into the grave: he was buried wearing his "Dracula" cape.

# Hillside Memorial Park

6001 Centinela Avenue

Before you even enter Hillside Memorial Park, you can catch a glimpse of one of its major attractions: the life-size statue of Al Jolson, bent down on one knee, arms opened wide in his characteristic pose. At the statue's feet is a waterfall, cascading 120 feet down the steep hillside.

Jolson, of course, entered movie history by appearing in *The Jazz Singer* (1927), the film that created a public demand for talking pictures. Originally, the role had been offered to the man who had performed it on the stage, George Jessel. Ironically, the two men are now buried within a few yards of each other.

Jessel was known as the "Toastmaster General" and became famous for his heartfelt (and numerous) eulogies. Presiding over one funeral, Jessel was extravagantly extolling the virtues of the dear departed when he happened to glance down into the open coffin. "Wait a minute," he exclaimed, "I *know* this guy!"

Jessel is interred in the Hillside Mausoleum, which provides a solemn backdrop to Jolson's theatrical monument. Another Jolson rival, Eddie Cantor, is also there. The drawers of the mausoleum are filled with notables: Jack Benny and his wife Mary Livingston Benny, comedian Dick Shawn, television stars David Janssen and Vic Morrow (who died while filming a sequence in the film *The Twilight Zone* in 1982), gangster Mickey Cohen, and comic singer Allan Sherman ("Hello Muddah, Hello Faddah...").

# Westwood Memorial Park

1218 Glendon Avenue

All cemeteries, by their nature, have tragic stories to tell. But Westwood Memorial seems more than usually filled with gifted people who died far too young. The crypt that attracts the most interest is, of course, that of Marilyn Monroe. Her death over three decades ago has not dimmed the public's fascination with this beautiful but troubled actress. Each year, on the anniversary of her death, a fan club gathers for a tribute service, and tourists visit her grave by the thousands annually.

But, while Marilyn is by far the most mythic of Westwood's tenants, she is not the only one who lived too short a life: Heather O'Rourke, the young star of the *Poltergeist* movies, was buried here after her death at the age of thirteen. Dominique Dunne, who played O'Rourke's older sister in *Poltergeist* (1982), was strangled by a jealous boyfriend (who was released from prison after only three years). Singer Minnie Riperton died of cancer at thirty-one. Dorothy Stratten, a former Playboy Playmate and promising actress, was murdered, at only twenty years of age, by her lover and "manager." And Natalie Wood, just forty-three, drowned in the waters off Catalina Island.

Darryl F. Zanuck, the head of 20th Century-Fox, is buried in Westwood Memorial, as is writer and producer Nunnally Johnson. The trenchant wit/composer/pianist Oscar Levant rests nearby. So do actors Donna Reed, Sebastian Cabot, and Victor Kilian, drummer Buddy Rich, songwriter Harry Warren, industrialist Armand Hammer and his family, and historians Will and Ariel Durant.

# Inglewood Park

720 East Florence Avenue

The subject of one of Hollywood's most enduring mysteries lies buried in this place of palm trees and beauty. Paul Bern, the husband of Jean Harlow, committed suicide (or was it murder?) only weeks after their wedding. Although several compelling theories have been set forth, no one has ever solved the case absolutely [see Chapter V: "Unsolved L.A. Mysteries"].

This modest memorial park is also the last earthly stopping place for Ferde Grofe, composer of "Grand Canyon Suite"; ventriloquist Edgar Bergen; and trapeze artist Lillian Leitzel, whose tomb is marked with a striking sculpture of a man embracing a winged woman who is flying from his arms.

"Our Gang's" Billy "Buckwheat" Thomas sleeps here not far from blues singer Willie Mae "Big Mama" Thornton. So do former World Heavyweight Boxing Champion James J. Jeffries and California Angels outfielder Lyman Bostock.

# Valhalla Memorial Park

10621 Victory Boulevard

The area around Burbank Airport is not the most scenic place on earth, and Valhalla is, overall, a rather bland, forgettable cemetery. However, television fans might want to make a pilgrimage there to pay respects to Bea Benaderet, the versatile comedienne whose roles ranged from the voice of Betty Rubble on *The Flintstones* to George and Gracie's neighbor Blanche on *The Burns and Allen Show* to lovable Kate Bradley, the mother of three knockouts who ran the Shady Rest Hotel on *Petticoat Junction.*

Our dear friend Mr. Hardy is also buried here. His grave is marked with a plaque, erected in 1977 by the Sons of the Desert, an international group of Laurel and Hardy enthusiasts, which reads: "Oliver Hardy, A Genius Of Comedy. His Talent Brought Joy And Laughter To All The World." And truer words were never carved on anything.

The Heritage Fountain is an impressive visual touch in a park with too few. A large, circular fountain, it features a layered pedestal in the center on which a classical figure stands. Wrestler Gorgeous George is buried nearby; so is actress Gail Russell. But kids of a certain middle age will particularly be interested in visiting the grave of Cliff Edwards, also known as Ukelele Ike. Doesn't sound familiar? Well, he was also the voice of an animated character named Jiminy Cricket.

## Home of Peace and Calvary

4334 Whittier Avenue

These two cemeteries are just across the street from each other. Home of Peace is a Jewish cemetery and Calvary is Catholic.

Reading the names on the markers at Home of Peace is like thumbing through a history of film and entertainment. "Uncle" Carl Laemmle, the founder and head of Universal Pictures, lies in the cemetery with numerous family members. (Laemmle was so notorious for nepotism at his studio—some seventy relatives were on the payroll—that Ogden Nash once wrote "Uncle Carl Laemmle has a very large faemmle.")

Louis B. Mayer, longtime head of M-G-M, is also in the park, as are at least two of the Warner Brothers: Harry and Jack.

For visitors with a Certain Sense of Humor (and your author freely pleads guilty), Home of Peace is notable for the presence of two of the greats: Jerome Howard, a.k.a. "Curly" of the Three Stooges, and his brother—and fellow Stooge—Shemp.

And the Funny Girl herself—Fanny Brice—is interred in the mausoleum, down the aptly named "Corridor of Memory."

Across the street at Calvary lie two of the famous Barrymores, Ethel and Lionel, as well as several noted stars of the Silent Screen, including Pola Negri, Mabel Normand, and Ramon Navarro.

Actor John Hodiak is here. So is comic Lou Costello, under his given name Louis Francis Cristillo.

But lest you think no one but movie folk are buried here, Calvary is also the last resting place of Henry T. Gage, the twentieth governor of California.

# Rosedale Cemetery

1831 West Washington

This pretty and restful spot is the home of several interesting, beautiful—sometimes bizarre—headstones, including a mausoleum shaped like a pyramid, a tombstone with the carving of a sinking ship (which is just how its occupant died), and another tombstone with a sleeping child carved on the top. It's a nice place to visit. However, Rosedale boasts only a few famous names.

Hattie McDaniel, the history-making actress (the first black performer to win an Academy Award; she was named Best Supporting Actress for *Gone With the*

*Wind*) sleeps here. So does the genius of jazz piano Art Tatum. Silent film actress Anna May Wong is interred near Tatum.

# Chapter XIV

# Sports in Los Angeles

Los Angeles is a sports lover's paradise. The sunny days, temperate climate, and invigorating smog make everyone, except for lazy authors, want to head outside and start sweating on purpose. There's a lot of outdoors in this city, and on a nice weekend, most of that wide open space is crowded with softball, football, and volleyball teams. Basketball courts are seldom vacant, and the beaches are filled not only with relaxed sun worshippers but with avid, active sports enthusiasts of every stripe.

Los Angeles is a great place to be a spectator of sports, too. I'm no great baseball fan, but one of my most enjoyable California afternoons was spent in the stands of Dodger Stadium, watching the game, chatting with a friend, and ingesting dangerous numbers of Dodger Dogs. As wonderful as the experience was for me, a non-fan, I imagine it must be something like heaven for those who really love the game.

There is a surprising variety of the kinds of sports practiced here, and the following listing offers many little corners of this sports paradise, whether you just want to watch or hop in and start spiking.

# Polo

Out at the beautiful Will Rogers State Park, at the far end of Sunset Boulevard at the edge of the Pacific, polo is still played on a regular basis, just as it was when Will himself used to live in the spacious house on the rise. Apparently, Rogers caught the polo bug from Our Gang and Laurel and Hardy producer Hal Roach in the twenties. Roach had seen the game being played at Midwick Country Club and became obsessed with it.

But not as obsessed as Rogers, who reportedly spent $100,000 creating a playing field just below his house, and another $50,000 on a stable of ponies. Soon, other Hollywood types were hooked on the sport: Darryl Zanuck, Walt Disney, Spencer Tracey, Jack Warner, and many others. As author Bruce Henstell writes, "The snobbishness traditionally associated with polo made it perfect for nouveau riche Hollywood."

# Baseball

If you live in Los Angeles and love baseball, it's almost a given that you're a Dodgers fan. The Dodgers entertain their hometown fans at beautiful Dodger Stadium, 1000 Elysian Park Avenue, (213) 224-1500. Of course, citizens of Anaheim will tell you that the Angels are no slouches, either, and that a game at Anaheim Stadium ("The Big A"), at 2000 South State College, (716) 634-2000, is just as invigorating as one at Dodger Stadium.

Old-timers, however, remember a couple of places to watch the game being played that, for sheer atmosphere, put both of those modern giants to shame. One was the old Wrigley Field, on Santa Barbara and 54th Street, where the Angels played in the thirties. Unlike its sister stadium in Chicago, L.A.'s Wrigley Field was equipped with lights for night baseball.

The Hollywood Stars played in various venues throughout the twenties and thirties, but in 1939 they got a spectacular new home in Gilmore Field at 7750 Beverly Boulevard. This beautiful Art Deco stadium is still fondly recalled by baseball fans of a certain age. But Gilmore Field, like the Stars, is nothing more than a memory. The Stars played their last game there in 1957. Gilmore Field was razed to make way for the old Pan Pacific Auditorium and, later, for CBS Television.

# Football

Pro football in Los Angeles owes its existance to Harold "Red" Grange, known to his millions of fans as "the Galloping Ghost." Grange generated an enormous following when he played college ball for the University of Illinois. When graduation loomed, a canny promotor named C.C. Pyle had an idea: he offered Red money—a lot of money—to keep on playing football for the struggling Chicago Bears.

With Red Grange's fame to boost them, the Bears drew a crowd of 70,000 when they played the Los Angeles Tigers at the L.A. Coliseum in 1927 (the Bears won 17-7). From that point on, pro football offered a serious threat to the supremacy of baseball as a national obsession.

Today, the Raiders play football at a different L.A. Coliseum, 3911 South Figueroa, (310) 322-5901 (this one was built in 1932 for the Olympics), and since 1980, the L.A. Rams have packed 'em in at Anaheim Stadium (see *Baseball* for address).

At least two college teams—USC and UCLA—have nearly as much popularity among Southern California fans as the Raiders and the Rams. They play home games at the Coliseum and at the Rose Bowl in Pasadena, (818) 825-2101.

In January 1995, it was announced that the Rams might not be a Los Angeles team for long. If negotiations between Rams owner Georgia Frontiere and business-man Stan Kroenke continue, the Rams will open the 1995 season at Busch Stadium in St. Louis, their new home. Eventually, a new 70,000-seat domed stadium will be built for the team. The move could bring the team an extra $20 million annually, which is nothing to sneeze at. But it will leave a big hole in the sports lives of thousands upon thousands of Los Angeles football fans.

# Tennis

Los Angeles' first tennis club was founded in 1884, and the sport has remained a favorite kind of upper class exercise ever since. There are both indoor and outdoor tennis courts at virtually every point in the city.

As a spectator sport, however, tennis has never made a particular splash in L.A.; the important matches are still centered on the East Coast and, of course, across the sea at Wimbledon.

# Golf

The first golf course in the city was built in 1897 near Pico and Alvarado. It eventually turned into the Los Angeles Country Club, which just goes to show you how an innocent piece of property can go wrong once rich guys start walking around on it wearing ugly pants.

Today, the city is crowded with both ugly pants and places to wear them while teeing off. Although most serious Los Angeles golfers prefer to head out to Palm Springs with its eighty courses, if you want to stay within the city limits you can try one of many country clubs such as Bel-Air, Wilshire, Lakeside, Brentwood, Brookside, or L.A. Country Club. Luminaries like W.C. Fields used to play some of these courses, and you're still apt to find a famous face making the rounds. Golf courses have always been a good place to do business, as well as a fine spot to get some sun and exercise. Listen closely to that foursome creeping up on you; you might hear a deal being made for *Jurassic Park II.*

## Surfing

If any single sport epitomizes the Southern California lifestyle, surfing would have to be the one. To those of us who grew up in other parts of the country, the music of the Beach Boys and those awful/wonderful Beach Party movies, starring Frankie Avalon and (be still my heart) Annette Funicello, created a picture of endless fun in or near the ocean. Malibu, Redondo Beach, Manhattan Beach, and Hermosa Beach have traditionally been top area surfing spots, but you'll find blond-haired hard-bodies riding the boards on just about any vacant wave up and down the coast.

If you want to learn more about the surprisingly rich heritage of California surfing (after all, it added the phrase, "Hang ten, Dude!" to the English language), you might find it fascinating to visit the Huntington Beach

International Surfing Museum, 411 Olive Avenue, (714) 960-3483.

# Basketball

Los Angeles has always been a baseball and football town; its mania for basketball is still relatively recent. When the Minnesota Lakers moved their headquarters to Los Angeles in 1960, nobody could have predicted what fierce loyalty the team would one day inspire among the great, near great, and not so great. In the 1980s, the Lakers won more NBA championships than any other team in the country and turned great players like Magic Johnson into bona fide sports legends.

The Lakers play at the Forum in Inglewood, Manchester Boulevard and Prairie Boulevard, (310) 419-3121, a stadium which was built for them. Tickets can be very hard to come by, but if you do get in, you can spend time-outs scanning the crowd for celebrities like Jack Nicholson, who attends virtually every Lakers game.

You can also catch the Kings, the city's hockey team, at the Forum. The phone number for tickets is (310) 419-3160. Hockey still seems a kind of an odd sport for Angelenos to have taken to heart, but the Kings are incredibly popular; it's not much easier to get tickets for their matches than for a Lakers game.

Los Angeles' other basketball team, the Clippers, play their home games at the Los Angeles Sports Arena, 3939 South Figueroa, (310) 748-8000. While the Clippers rarely draw Laker-sized crowds, they have a large and loyal following. If you have a spur-of-the-moment desire to catch a basketball game, you'll definitely find it easier to get Clippers tickets. And, except for the fact that you probably won't see Jack Nicholson there, you'll have just as swell a time.

*Los Angeles Memorial Coliseum*

# The Olympics (1932 and 1984)

When it was learned in the early twenties that Los Angeles would host the 1932 Olympics—the Tenth Modern Olympiad—it seemed like quite a feather in the city's cap. Little did anyone know that by the time 1932 rolled around, the country—L.A. included—would be mired neck-deep in the Great Depression. That might have given some cities pause, but by gum we don't quit in L.A., not unless we have a play or pay contract.

Immediately, the powers that be began planning cost-cutting measures, including the construction of an Olympic Village in Baldwin Hills where 2,000 male athletes from all nations could live in peace and harmony. Female athletes didn't have to live in peace and harmony. They were put up in hotels.

An Olympic Auditorium—now called the Memorial Coliseum—was built at the corner of Olympic and Grand avenues. Capable of holding approximately 100,000 people, the Coliseum hosted a spectacular Olympic opening day on July 30, 1932.

Of all the spectacularly gifted athletes competing in the 1932 Olympics, perhaps none was so versatile and accomplished as Mildred "Babe" Didrikson. Then eighteen-year-old Didrikson excelled in the javelin, shot put, high jump, long jump, and hurdles. She created a new Olympic and world record when she threw the javelin for 143 feet 4 inches and did it again by jumping 80-meter hurdles in 11.7 seconds. Didrikson broke a third Olympic and world record with her high jump. But officials disqualified her for "diving" over the bar and awarded her the silver medal. The rule against her jumping style was repealed the next year.

The 1932 Olympics saw the introduction of at least two innovations that would become a permanent part of Olympic ritual: it was the first time that a victory stand was constructed where the medal winners would receive their awards as their national anthems played; and, for the first time, electric photo-timing devices were used to help determine winners in particularly close races.

In 1984 the Olympics returned to Los Angeles and were again played in the Memorial Coliseum. This time there was no Depression to cut corners, and the entire cultural, political, and athletic community of Los Angeles turned out in full force to celebrate the event. The Los Angeles International Airport received a much-needed facelift. There were theater festivals, special museum and gallery events, Olympic-related concerts, and celebrations of all kinds.

In 1932 the Olympic committee did not okay marketing tie-ins of any kind, save the sale of an "Olympic Emblem." By 1984 times had changed and marketing giants like Arco, McDonald's, Coca Cola, Mars, and many others bought a piece of the Olympic pie.

The games themselves received worldwide attention, benefitting from television and other technologies that had not been available fifty years earlier. The spectacular success of the 1984 Olympics proved that Los Angeles was not simply the center of the entertainment universe—it is also a world-class city on every level.

## The Los Angeles Marathon

The first Los Angeles Marathon was run in 1986 and soon developed into the world's third largest such event. The 26.2-mile course begins on Figueroa Street near the L.A. Coliseum, heads northeast across the Hollywood Freeway to Sunset Boulevard, then west on Hollywood Boulevard, south on Rossmore, east on Wilshire, southwest on Crenshaw, and east on Exposition Boulevard, to bring the tired runners back to the starting point.

The Tenth Marathon, run on March 5, 1995, was preceded by a two-day extravaganza at the L.A. Convention Center, "The Quality of Life Expo," which offered seminars, demonstrations, and a staggering variety of athletic gear. A "last supper," held on the eve of the race, attracted over 5,000 people to the Hollywood Paladium to carbo-load on pasta, potatoes, rolls, fruits, and salads.

In 1995, for the first time, the L.A. Marathon was accompanied by a bike marathon in which 15,000 bikers followed the same route as the runners.

The biggest winners of the marathon are the fifty-two charities, from the Red Cross to Hollygrove Children's Home, which raise money through pledges. Between 1988 and 1995, over $5.2 million was raised to help feed, clothe, and lend support to the city's less fortunate.

*Los Angeles Magazine* (March 1995) profiled ten runners who had participated in all ten of the marathons to date. One man, Dutch Benedetti, eighty, ran his first marathon at sixty-eight. "I usually win my age category," Dutch said, "even with Alzheimer's. I feel great when I cross the finish line...my wife says I'm usually the only one smiling."

## Chapter XV

# L.A. Trivia

- Los Angeles was incorporated in 1850.
- Los Angeles' first tennis club was formed in 1884.
- In 1877 Don William Wolfskill shipped the first California oranges back East.
- In 1958 the first eight stars were placed in the Hollywood Walk of Fame: Olive Borden, Ernest Torrence, Joanne Woodward, Preston Foster, Ronald Colman, Louise Fazenda, Edward Sedgwick, and Burt Lancaster.
- Los Angeles' last fire horse ran in 1929.
- In 1995 Ed Lange was voted Citizen of the Year by the Topanga Chamber of Commerce. Lange is the founder of Elysium Fields, Los Angeles County's only nudist colony.
- The Beverly Wilshire Hotel offers a "Pretty Woman" package for amorous couples who want to pretend to be Julia Roberts and Richard Gere.
- In 1855 Los Angeles Mayor Stephen G. Foster resigned his office long enough to join a lynch mob. As soon as the unfortunate culprit was swinging from a tree, the mayor resumed his duties.

- The first completed freeway in the area was the Pasadena Freeway (also known as the Arroyo Seco Parkway), built between 1934 and 1941.

- Contrary to legend, Roy Rogers' horse Trigger has not been stuffed. His hide has been mounted on a fiberglass frame. And he looks "mahvelous."

- "Deadman's Curve," made famous in a 1964 song by Jan and Dean, is on Sunset Boulevard just west of UCLA.

- There is a herd of bison on Catalina Island.

- The Hollywood Chamber of Commerce has been trying to erect a Hollywood Museum since 1959, but it hasn't been built yet.

- However, Debbie Reynolds' Hollywood Museum opened on Saturday, April 1, 1995—in Las Vegas.

- Zsa Zsa Gabor was arrested in 1989 for slapping a police officer at the corner of Olympic and La Cienega.

- There are over twice as many pool halls in Los Angeles as golf courses.

- When Union Station was built in 1939, workers found a maze of tunnels and dungeons dug by former inhabitants of Chinatown.

- One name is misspelled on the Hollywood Walk of Fame. "Morris Diller" is supposed to be famed director Mauritz Stiller.

- In 1897 Sam Sturgis, a bicycle maker, built the first automobile ever seen in Los Angeles.

- Norma Desmond's mansion in *Sunset Boulevard* (1950) was actually located at 641 Irving.

- 4.5 million traffic tickets are issued each year.

- Famed Western marshal Wyatt Earp died on Seventeenth Street in 1929.

- There is no such address as 77 Sunset Strip.

- In 1910, concerned by the horrendous speed of automobiles, officials instituted a speed limit of 6 miles per hour downtown and 30 miles per hour everywhere else.

- The ghost of Lon Chaney used to be sighted regularly on a bus stop bench at the corner of Hollywood and Vine. When the bench was removed, the Man of a Thousand Faces left, too.

- Clara Blandick, "Aunt Em" from *The Wizard of Oz* (1939), committed suicide in the Shelton Apartments, 1735 N. Wilcox, by pulling a plastic bag over her head.

- In 1542 Juan Cabrillo, the first European to set eyes on what would become Los Angeles, called the area Bahia de los Fumos—Bay of the Smokes—because of the smog.

- For a donation of $1 million, Los Angeles will name one of its libraries after you.

- Mickey Mouse has a star on the Hollywood Walk of Fame. But Donald Duck doesn't.

- The gymnasium floor that opens to reveal a swimming pool in *It's a Wonderful Life* (1946) still exists at Beverly Hills High School, 255 S. Lasky Drive.

- The country's first air show was held in Dominguez Hills in Los Angeles County in 1910. The Wright Brothers didn't show, but every other notable name in aviation was there.

- Ninety-five percent of all film and video pornography is produced in the San Fernando Valley.

- There are over 800 private schools in Greater Los Angeles.

- The first Tournament of Roses Parade in Pasadena was held in 1890.

- Bela Lugosi was buried in his Dracula cape.

- The L.A. Air Pollution Board was formed in 1948.

- The impossibly steep steps, up which Laurel and Hardy labored to deliver a piano in *The Music Box* (1933), are located at 923-27 Vendome Street. A plaque once marked the spot, but it was stolen.

- Northridge, the city hardest hit by the earthquake of 1994, is also where Richard Pryor once set himself on fire while freebasing cocaine.

- The city of Tarzana was named after *Tarzan, King of the Apes*. The property was once owned by Tarzan's creator, Edgar Rice Burroughs.

- The city of Burbank is 699 feet above sea level.

- There are nine homes and buildings in Los Angeles which were designed by Frank Lloyd Wright.

- According to AA, Al-Anon, and AlaTeen attendance records, there are more drunks in West L.A. than in any other area of the city.

- Western Costume operates a thrift shop at 11041 Vanowen Street in North Hollywood where you can buy old movie costumes and props.

- Marilyn Monroe posed for her famous nude calender photographs in photographer Tom Kelley's studio at 736 N. Seward.

- In 1920 Los Angeles officially became a bigger city than San Francisco.

- "La Brea" is Spanish for "tar." Hence, very little imagination was used in naming the La Brea Tar Pits.

- Until 1934 a caretaker lived in a little shack behind the first "L" in the "Hollywoodland" sign.

- The "Sigalert," a notice that there is trouble on one of the freeways, was named for Lloyd Sigmon who came up with the device in the first place (while waiting in traffic, no doubt).

- Gene Autry has five stars on the Hollywood Walk of Fame—more than anyone else.

- Gold was discovered near the San Fernando Mission in 1842, years before the Sutter's Mill discovery that caused the Gold Rush of 1849.

- In 1928 the *Los Angeles Times* became the first newspaper to be delivered in part by airplane.

- In 1905 rainmaker Charles Mallory Hatfield was awarded $1,000 from the Los Angeles Chamber of Commerce for producing eighteen inches of rain in the first four months of the year.

- In 1957 waitress Beverly Nina Avery obtained her sixteenth divorce—a record, even in L.A.

- The first Super Bowl was played at Memorial Coliseum on January 15, 1967. The Green Bay Packers beat the Kansas City Chiefs 35 - 10.

- Janis Joplin died at the Landmark Motel, 7047 Franklin Avenue.

- Jayne Mansfield had a heart-shaped swimming pool. Liberace's was shaped like a piano.

- Los Angeles City Hall, at 200 N. Spring Street, had a long-running television role as the "Daily Planet Building" on *The Adventures of Superman*.

- Beverly Garland, once a co-star on *My Three Sons*, bought a Howard Johnson Hotel in Studio City and renamed it the Beverly Garland.

- There are more liquor stores in Whittier/Downey than in any other part of Los Angeles.

- The Culver City sets for King Kong (1933) were torched for the "burning of Atlanta" sequence in *Gone With the Wind* (1939).

- John F. Kennedy and Marilyn Monroe kept romantic rendezvous at a beach house at 625 Palisades Beach Road.

- When Rin-Tin-Tin died in 1932, he was buried in the backyard of his home at 1352 Clubview Drive.

- Hollywood's first Christmas Parade was held in 1928. For many years thereafter, during the Christmas season, Hollywood Boulevard was renamed Santa Claus Lane.

- Clark Gable's false teeth were made by a dentist in the Equitable building at the corner of Hollywood and Vine.

- A star on the Hollywood Walk of Fame will set you back $3,500.

- Marilyn Monroe met Joe DiMaggio on a blind date at the Villa Nova Restaurant, 9015 Sunset Boulevard.

- The first Automatic Teller Machine (ATM) was installed at the Civic Center branch of Surety National Bank on April 27, 1971. It is not clear how humanity survived prior to this.

# Acknowledgments

Of all the books I've written, this has been one of the most enjoyable to research. I get a real kick out of Los Angeles and love driving around looking for all those interesting hidden places. Happily, I've had some wonderful people helping me find what I'm looking for, and I am most grateful to them all for lending a hand.

Chief among these is my great pal Thomas W. Holland. He's as enthusiastic about Los Angeles as I am (and my wife thinks he's just as crazy as she thinks I am) and we have shared some great times tooling around the city, maps in hand, searching for signs of the past, from the old Mack Sennett studio to the Formosa Cafe. More crucially, Tom gave me access to his impressive library of books about Los Angeles, which has proved absolutely invaluable to me. Maybe I could have written this book without Tom's help but it would have been much harder, more time-consuming, and a lot less fun.

Other friends helped out, too. I want to offer my sincere thanks to Leith Adams, Warner Bros.; Julie Gibson Barton; Bob Birchard; Quince Buteau; Craig Covner; Sam Gill; the immortal Mary Goldman; Karen Morley Gough; Howard Green, Walt Disney Company; Scott MacQueen, Walt Disney Company; Nina Rosenstand; Doug Roth; Dianne Stultz and Russell Stultz, Wordware Publishing; and Pete, Jake and Molly, California dogs through and through.

And finally, my endless gratitude and love go to my beautiful wife, Claire McCulloch Thompson. She doesn't much care for Los Angeles, but she puts up with it for my sake. I am thankful to her for this and the many, many other things she has done for me.

# A Los Angeles Bibliography

It isn't possible—or even desirable—to list every publication I referred to while researching *Los Angeles Uncovered*; it would have to include hundreds of books, magazines, and newspapers. But if this book inspires you to seek out more details on the people, places, and events discussed so fleetingly in these pages, the following bibliography should provide a great deal of information and enjoyment.

Bearchell, Charles A. and Larry D. Fried, *The San Fernando Valley Then and Now*. Northridge, California: Windsor Publications, Inc., 1988.

Brownlow, Kevin, *The Parade's Gone By*. New York: Alfred A. Knopf, 1969.

Brownlow, Kevin, *Hollywood: The Pioneers*. London: Collins, 1979.

Carr, Harry, *Los Angeles: City of Dreams*. New York: D. Appleton-Century Company, Inc., 1935.

Culbertson, Judi and Tom Randall, *Permanent Californians: An Illustrated Guide to the Cemeteries of California*. Chelsea, Vermont: Chelsea Green Publishing Company, 1989.

Heimann, Jim, *Out With the Stars: Hollywood Nightlife in the Golden Era*. New York: Abbeville Press, 1985.

Henstell, Bruce, *Sunshine and Wealth: Los Angeles in the Twenties and Thirties*. San Francisco: Chronicle Books.

Holzer, Hans, *Westghosts: The Psychic World of California*. Chicago: The Swallow Press, 1980.

Hoover, Mildred Brooke, Hero Eugene Rensch and Ethel Grace Rensch, *Historic Spots in California (Third Edition revised by William N. Abeloe)*. Stanford, California: Stanford University Press, 1966.

Hopkins, Jerry, *The L.A. Book of Lists*. Los Angeles: Price/Stern/Sloan, 1987.

Jacobson, Laurie and Marc Wanamaker, *Hollywood Haunted: A Ghostly Tour of Filmland*. Santa Monica: Angel City Press, 1994.

Jorgensen, Lawrence C., *The San Fernando Valley Past and Present*. Los Angeles: Pacific Rim Research, 1982.

Kaplan, Sam Hall, *L.A. Lost & Found: An Architectural History of Los Angeles*. New York: Crown Publishers, Inc., 1987.

Kennelly, Joe and Roy Hankey, *Sunset Boulevard: America's Dream Street*. Burbank, California: Darwin Publications, 1981.

Lamparski, Richard, *Lamparski's Hidden Hollywood*. New York: Fireside/Simon and Schuster, 1981.

May, Antoinette, *Haunted Houses of California*. San Carlos, California: Wide World Publishing/Tetra, 1990.

Munn, Michael, *The Hollywood Murder Case Book*. New York: St. Martin's Press, 1987.

Myers, Arthur, *The Ghostly Register: A Guide to Haunted America*. New York: Dorset Press, 1986.

Ramsey, Terry, *A Million and One Nights: A History of the Motion Picture Through 1925*. New York: Simon & Schuster, Inc., 1926. Touchstone reprint, 1986.

Reavill, Gil, *Hollywood and the Best of Los Angeles*. Oakland, California: Compass American Guides, Inc., 1994.

Schessler, Ken, *This is Hollywood*. La Verne, California: Ken Schessler Productions, 1978. 11th Edition, 1993.

Starr, Kevin, *Inventing the Dream: California Through the Progressive Era*. Oxford: Oxford University Press, 1985.

Sturges, Preston, *Preston Sturges by Preston Sturges*. New York: Simon and Schuster, 1990.

Thompson, Frank, et al, *Between Action and Cut: Five American Directors*. Metuchen, New Jersey: The Scarecrow Press, 1985.

Torrence, Bruce T., *Hollywood: The First Hundred Years*. New York: New York Zoetrope, 1982.

Ward, Elizabeth and Alain Silver, *Raymond Chandler's Los Angeles*. Woodstock, New York: The Overlook Press, 1987.

Wilcock, John ed., *Insight Guides Los Angeles*. Boston: Houghton Mifflin Company, 1993.

Williams, Greg, et al, *The Story of Hollywoodland*. Hollywood: Papavasilopoulos Press, 1992.

# About the Author

Frank Thompson is a writer and film historian, the author of books, scripts, and hundreds of articles, reviews, and interviews in newspapers and magazines. His books include: *Robert Wise: A Bio-Bibliography* (Greenwood, 1995), *Lost Movies* (Citadel, 1995), *Tim Burton's "The Nightmare Before Christmas"* (Hyperion, 1993), *Alamo Movies* (Republic of Texas Press, 1994), *Between Action and Cut: Five American Directors* (Scarecrow Press, 1985), and *William A. Wellman* (Scarecrow Press, 1983). The Wellman biography was issued in a new edition in 1993 by the Filmoteca Espanol in conjunction with a Wellman tribute at the San Sebastian Film Festival, at which Thompson was a guest of honor.

Thompson has written scripts for the American Movie Classics cable channel. He acted as associate producer and appears onscreen in *Wild Bill Wellman* (Coyote Films, 1995), a documentary about the career of William A. Wellman.

Feature film scripts include *The Last Stand*. Television scripts include episodes of *Hollywood Babylon* (1992), *Frank Capra: A Personal Remembrance* (Vid-America, 1992), and *The Making of "It's a Wonderful Life"* (Republic Pictures, 1991).

Thompson has contributed to several film encyclopedias and is a regular writer for magazines such as *American Cinematographer*, *American Film*, *Film Comment*, *The Hollywood Reporter*, *The Disney Channel Magazine*, *Sight and Sound*, *Tower Pulse!*, and *Texas Monthly*.

He has also written for many newspapers, notably *The Atlanta Journal & Constitution*, *The Miami Herald*, *The Philadelphia Inquirer*, *The San Francisco Chronicle*, *The Boston Globe*, and *The San Antonio Express News*.

Frank Thompson lives in Burbank, California, which is near Los Angeles but a lot quieter.

# Index